BOSTON 1775

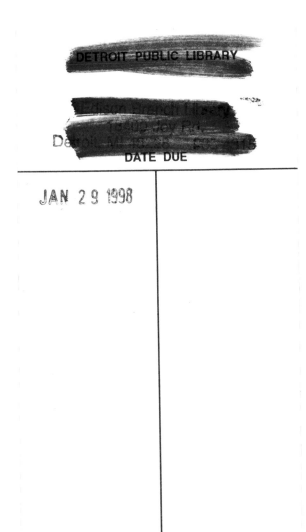

APR 1996

ED

BOSTON 1775

THE SHOT HEARD AROUND THE WORLD

BRENDAN MORRISSEY

First published in Great Britain in 1995 by
Osprey, an imprint of Reed Consumer Books
Limited, Michelin House, 81 Fulham Road,
London SW3 6RB and Auckland, Melbourne,
Singapore and Toronto.

ISBN 1 85532 362 1

Military Editor: Lee Johnson.
Edited by Tony Holmes.
Designed by Paul Kime.

Colour bird's eye view illustrations by
Peter Harper.
Cartography by Micromap. *Wargaming the
Boston Campaign* by Brendan Morrissey.

Fimset in Great Britain.
Printed through Bookbuilders Ltd.,
Hong Kong.

DEDICATION

To my grandparents, George and Ellen, and to my wife, Nora.

AUTHOR'S NOTE

While acknowledging any historical and philosophical inaccuracy, for
the sake of brevity and simplicity, the white inhabitants of the 13
colonies are referred to as either 'Americans' or 'Loyalists' (according to
allegiance), and the King's troops as 'regulars'.

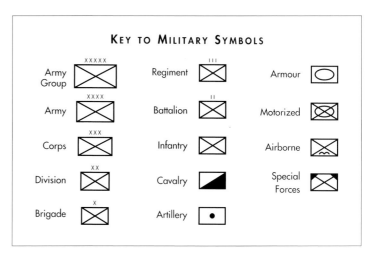

KEY TO MILITARY SYMBOLS

Army Group	xxxxx	Regiment	ııı
Army	xxxx	Battalion	ıı
Corps	xxx	Infantry	
Division	xx	Cavalry	
Brigade	x	Artillery	
		Armour	
		Motorized	
		Airborne	
		Special Forces	

If you would like to receive more information about
Osprey Military books, The Osprey Messenger is a regular
newsletter which contains articles, new title information
and special offers. To join free of charge
please write to:

**Osprey Military Messenger,
PO Box 5, Rushden,
Northants NN10 6YX**

CONTENTS

COLONIAL NORTH AMERICA C.1775

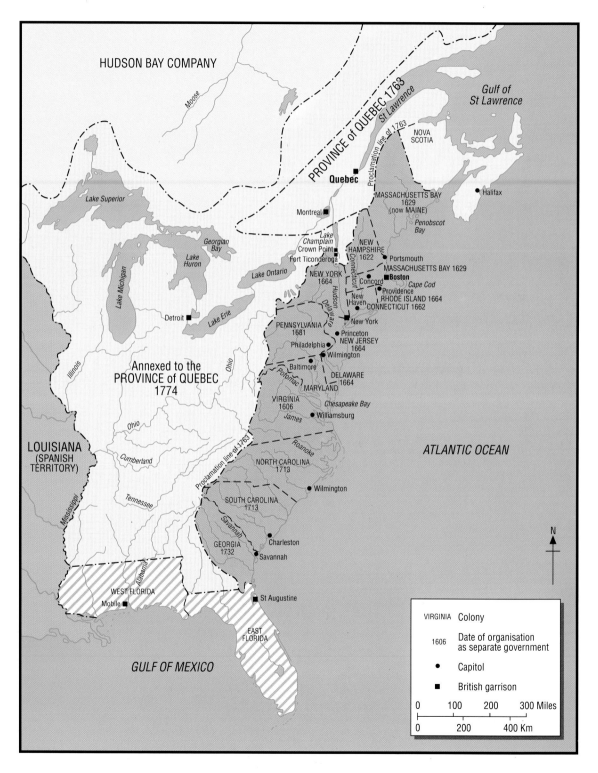

HUDSON BAY COMPANY

Moose

PROVINCE of QUEBEC 1763

St Lawrence

Gulf of
St Lawrence

Proclamation line of 1763

NOVA
SCOTIA

Quebec

Halifax

Lake Superior

Montreal

MASSACHUSETTS BAY
1629
(now MAINE)

Penobscot
Bay

Georgian
Bay

Lake
Champlain
Crown Point
Fort Ticonderoga

NEW
HAMPSHIRE
1622

Portsmouth

Lake
Huron

Lake Michigan

Lake Ontario

NEW YORK
1664

Connecticut

MASSACHUSETTS BAY 1629
Boston

Concord

Cape Cod

Detroit

Lake Erie

Hudson

New
Haven

Providence
RHODE ISLAND 1664
CONNECTICUT 1662

Delaware

New York

Illinois

PENNSYLVANIA
1681

Princeton
NEW JERSEY
1664

Ohio

Philadelphia

Wilmington

Annexed to the
PROVINCE of QUEBEC
1774

Baltimore

Potomac

DELAWARE
1664

MARYLAND

Ohio

VIRGINIA
1606

Chesapeake Bay

James

Williamsburg

LOUISIANA
(SPANISH
TERRITORY)

Cumberland

Proclamation line of 1763

Roanoke

ATLANTIC OCEAN

NORTH CAROLINA
1713

Tennessee

Wilmington

Mississippi

SOUTH CAROLINA
1713

Savannah

GEORGIA
1732

Charleston

Savannah

N

Alabama

WEST FLORIDA
Mobile

St Augustine

EAST
FLORIDA

GULF OF MEXICO

VIRGINIA	Colony
1606	Date of organisation as separate government
●	Capitol
■	British garrison

| 0 | 100 | 200 | 300 Miles |
| 0 | 200 | | 400 Km |

THE ROAD TO WAR

King George III (1760-1820) was exceptionally pious for the times, and was only 22 when he took the throne, but within five years showed symptoms of the illness that blighted his later life. Often depicted as a tyrant, he had firm views on Parliament's right to tax, but opposed moves to crush his American subjects, restraining the 'hawks' among his ministers on more than one occasion. (National Portait Gallery, London)

For over 200 years, historians have sought the moment when a revolution in America became inevitable. If one existed, it was probably the founding of the American colonies 150 years earlier, and 3000 miles away, by Englishmen seeking religious or political independence. By 1775, their descendants were *de facto* managers of their own affairs, and it was probably Parliament's lack of involvement before 1763 that had kept the peace. While they might claim rights as 'Englishmen', many of the inhabitants were, by the 1760s, third or fourth generation colonists, and thought of themselves (if only unconsciously) as different from their British cousins – in fact, as Americans.

On King George III's accession, in October 1760, Great Britain was the pre-eminent colonial power on the sub-continent, following Wolfe's victory at Quebec and Montreal's surrender to Amherst. Yet, the end of seven decades of continuous warfare brought not stability, but confrontation that would, within 15 years, result in armed rebellion.

COLONIAL AMERICA

Between Canada and Florida lay 13 colonies: New Hampshire, Massachusetts, Rhode Island and Connecticut (known collectively as New England), New York, New Jersey, Pennsylvania, Delaware, Maryland, Virginia, North and South Carolina and Georgia. Nine were Crown colonies with governors appointed in London, and of the others, Maryland and Pennsylvania were, in essence, privately owned, while Connecticut and Rhode Island were chartered colonies with elected governors.

In 1760, the population was about 1,600,000, excluding Indians, but including 325,000 slaves, of whom 95 per cent lived in rural communities. By 1775 this figure had risen to 2,250,000 (including 500,000 slaves), compared with a population of 8,000,000 in Great Britain and Ireland.

The vast majority of whites were of British stock, the remainder being mainly German, Dutch or Swiss. Many had emigrated to escape persecution, or criminal prosecution, but despite this volatile mixture, rebellion was unlikely because the cultural differences between the Colonies resulted in a lack of consensus on almost everything. In fact, there was constant bickering, often violent, between neighbouring Colonies, and it would

need something exceptional to bring this disjointed group together – unfortunately, the King's ministers were, unwittingly, about to do just that.

COLONIAL POLICY

Until 1763, few British governments had a cohesive policy for governing the Colonies and, inevitably, the colonial assemblies gradually usurped the powers of Crown and Parliament. Even defence was primarily a responsibility of the Colonists, with British aid being limited to naval or logistical support, so the militia (though differing from colony to colony) became a substantially different force from its English equivalent

But while the Colonists assumed Great Britain would revert to its policy of non-government, Parliament saw the crowning of a new King as an ideal opportunity to consolidate political control. The Proclamation of 1763 fixed the Colonies' western boundaries, limited migration and stopped lucrative land speculation. Enforced by a chain of forts, whose commanding officers governed the local population, the continued presence of regular troops led some Colonists to resurrect the old English bogey of standing armies as a threat to liberty.

Like all British colonies, those in North America existed to serve British interests. The Seven Years War had left Great Britain with a massive national debt, and with 10,000 troops in America, plus English taxpayers paying 25 shillings to an American's six-pence, the King's chief minister, George Grenville, felt it was time to share the tax burden more evenly. When the Colonies refused to co-operate, they were taxed. The Stamp Act, which merely imposed duties that had existed in England for years, particularly outraged the Colonists, and mobs calling themselves 'Sons of Liberty' rampaged through Boston and New York. The troops sent to end this violence became increasingly unpopular themselves; in New York, a Quartering Act allowed them to occupy private property if barracks were unavailable (a common enough measure in England). Four regiments were sent to Boston and were immediately subjected to political intimidation, whilst fights between soldiers and civilians became increasingly common, especially when the former offered themselves as cheap labour.

ABOVE *Samuel Adams (1722-1803), shabby in appearance and deed, whose failures included the unique achievement (for those times) of accumulating massive debts whilst serving as a tax collector. Apart from founding the first Committee of Correspondence (quickly adopted by other colonies) to co-ordinate opposition, he made few positive contributions. Adept at creating confrontation, someone very similar was seen directing the crowd at the 'Boston Massacre', and he undoubtedly had a hand in the outbreak of hostilities at Lexington. (Museum of Fine Arts, Boston)*

The Boston Tea Party was just one of several similar incidents throughout the colonies, and it was inspired as much (if not more) by the financial ruin facing wealthy smugglers, like John Hancock, as by any fine political principles. It can hardly have improved the quality of the local water – a town council edict of the 1660s forbade the dumping of refuse in the harbour, and warned against swimming in the foul water because of the level of pollution. (Anne S K Brown Military Collection, Brown University Library)

On 5 March 1770, a crowd attacked a sentry outside the Custom House in Boston. The guard was called out and, in the confusion, opened fire, killing five of the mob and wounding five more. Despite a vicious Whig propaganda campaign, calling it the 'Boston massacre' and depicting it as a typically brutal attack on peaceful civilians, when the soldiers went on trial all but two (who were branded and dismissed from the service) were acquitted. Outside Boston, there were calls to end 'mobbing' and disband the 'Sons of Liberty'.

Lord North, who succeeded Grenville and was much closer to the King, preferred a policy of conciliation. He immediately repealed every tax, except that on tea. The ensuing lull was deceptive and suggested that the worst was over, but in June 1772 the Royal Navy schooner HMS *Gaspee* was burnt by Rhode Island smugglers, and British tea, dubbed 'the beverage of traitors', was boycotted. North sought to defuse the situation (and thus save the failing East India Company) by reducing the tax, until it was cheaper than smuggled tea, but Boston radical, Samuel Adams, and other prominent smugglers continually emphasised the tax question, and in December 1773 organised the 'Boston Tea Party' (one of several in the Colonies).

Parliament's response – known in America as the Intolerable, or Coercive Acts – included the closure of Boston's port, royal control of public appointments in Massachusetts, a new Quartering Act and the Quebec Act (awakening fears of a Catholic conspiracy). The Acts, particularly, drew the Colonies together: aid flooded into Boston and in September 1774 a Congress held in Philadelphia was attended by representatives from every colony except Georgia.

COLONIAL NEW ENGLAND C.1775

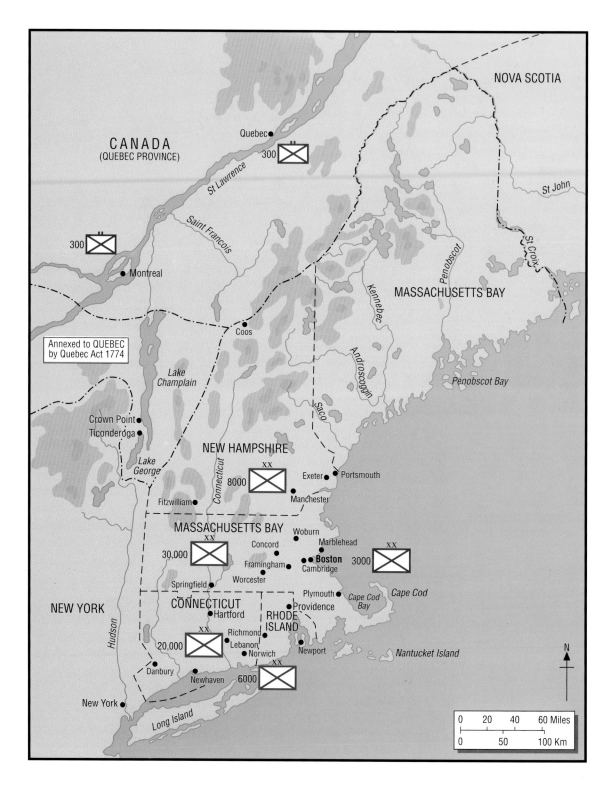

NOVA SCOTIA

CANADA
(QUEBEC PROVINCE)

Quebec

300

St Lawrence

St John

300

Montreal

Saint Francois

Kennebec

Penobscot

St Croix

MASSACHUSETTS BAY

Coos

Annexed to QUEBEC
by Quebec Act 1774

Lake
Champlain

Androscoggin

Penobscot Bay

Crown Point
Ticonderoga

Saco

Lake
George

NEW HAMPSHIRE

Connecticut

8000   XX

Exeter   Portsmouth

Fitzwilliam

Manchester

MASSACHUSETTS BAY   Woburn

Concord   Marblehead

30,000   XX

Framingham   Boston   3000   XX

Worcester   Cambridge

Springfield

Plymouth   Cape Cod
Bay   Cape Cod

NEW YORK

CONNECTICUT   Providence

RHODE
ISLAND

Hartford

Hudson

Richmond

20,000   XX   Lebanon

Norwich   Newport   Nantucket Island

Danbury

N

Newhaven   6000   XX

New York

Long Island

| 0 | 20 | 40 | 60 Miles |
| 0 | 50 | | 100 Km |

THE SEAT OF WAR

Lieutenant General the Honourable Thomas Gage (1719-1787) was anonymous as a soldier, and made little impact on the military events around Boston, despite his considerable personal qualities. Failure to control the Bostonians led his men to christen him 'Old Tom' and 'Granny Gage', and without underestimating the difficulties he faced, the atmosphere of inefficiency and inactivity that pervaded his headquarters reflected his own indecision. Like many British officers, he had an American wife. (Firle Collection, Firle Place, Sussex)

Massachusetts had taken the lead in opposing Parliamentary sovereignty and, not surprisingly, it was singled out for punishment. Lieutenant General Thomas Gage, commander-in-chief in North America since 1763, became Governor of Massachusetts, and was charged with enforcing the Intolerable Acts. However, the General Assembly frustrated him by forming a Provincial Congress, based in Concord (20 miles west of Boston), with John Hancock as president. This in turn became the *de facto* government of Massachusetts, leaving Gage ruling only Boston.

BOSTON IN 1775

Boston was the third largest town in North America, with 16,000 inhabitants, and stood on a peninsula connected to the mainland by a neck just wide enough to cross at high tide. The harbour, large enough to be strategically significant, and central to Boston's economy, was formed by a chain of islands stretching out to sea, guarded by reefs and ledges. Its main channel, protected by Castle William, was narrow and awkward, with seasonal tides and currents making entry difficult. The inner roads were shallow, with tidal islands, mud flats and marshes, criss-crossed by tricky channels known only to the locals (even Royal Navy ships constantly ran aground). In winter fog and fierce storms were common, and the harbour often froze over.

South, across Boston Neck, lay Roxbury and Dorchester Neck, a peninsula whose heights overlooked the harbour and Castle William. To the west was the Back Bay (which could hold smaller vessels) and the mouth of the Charles River, while inland lay Cambridge and Harvard University.

North west of Boston was Charlestown, a largely rural peninsula one-and-a-half miles long, connected by a neck ten yards across at high tide, and a mill dam wide enough to cross in single file. Charlestown stood at the south east corner (facing Boston) with three hills behind it – Bunker's Hill, nearest the neck, Breed's Hill 200 yards above the town and Moulton's (or Morton's) Hill to the north east. Beyond was the Mystic River, leading nowhere and full of awkward shallows, while north and east lay several islands, sparsely inhabited and used mainly for grazing.

Militarily, Boston had no value beyond its harbour. There were no

View of the South End of Boston in New England America, & of the N... taken from the Hill N E of the Common... By...

objectives within striking distance, and any advance would be extremely difficult in a countryside favouring irregular tactics with many hills, woods, rivers and ravines, but few roads. The only reason for soldiers to be there, as both sides well knew, was to control the towns-people.

GAGE'S DILEMMA

Despite an uncharacteristic boast that he could subdue Boston with four regiments, by August 1774 Gage was finding twice that number, plus artillery, inadequate. The inhabitants, when not attacking officers and men (especially after Gage forbade them to wear swords), would encourage them to desert, steal their weapons, or sell them drink (often bad). Magistrates fined soldiers disproportionate sums for trivial offences, while denying them justice against civilians, unless they had civilian witnesses. Closing the port made thousands redundant, but they refused to work for Gage or the Royal Navy, preferring to watch the troops and report their movements, making secrecy impossible for the British.

But Gage, too, had his spies (including Dr Benjamin Church, a trusted member of the Provincial Congress, and Major General William Brattle of the Massachusetts militia) and was aware of the Provincial Congress's plans. On 1 September, he sent 260 men to seize the King's powder in Charlestown powderhouse and two brass cannon in Cambridge, catching the militia completely by surprise. Angered by stories of atrocities (which were completely false), over 4000 militia assembled in Cambridge the next

Drawn by a Royal Navy officer in 1764, these views depict the south and north ends of Boston and the surrounding countryside (a third drawing shows the islands in the harbour). At left is the South End and Boston Neck, with Dorchester Heights behind. In the left foreground is Boston Common; the round structure is the powder magazine. To the right the view continues round to Charlestown Neck, with Breed's and Bunker Hills behind Charlestown, with Boston's North End at the extreme right. In the Back Bay – centre foreground – are fishing boats, essential to the local economy. (Bostonian Society, Old State House, Boston)

day, and forced the two judges to resign; two days later, 6000 militia in Worcester stopped the courts sitting. Gage took the advice of local Tories and sent no troops to oppose them, but strengthened the fortifications across Boston Neck.

Shocked by Gage's weapons seizure, the Provincial Congress created a system of 'alarm riders' to rouse the countryside every time the regulars left Boston, and reorganised the militia. Units of 'minute men' were created, ready to march at a moment's notice to oppose the regulars, and Committees of Safety and Supplies were set up, with authority to mobilise the militia and seize stores.

On 8 September another force sent to retrieve cannon from harbour fortifications in Charlestown found that the guns were gone. All over Massachusetts, and even in Boston itself, cannon, stores and munitions began to disappear from public arsenals. During October, Gage received reinforcements from New York, Halifax and Quebec raising his strength to about 3000 men.*

Other colonies followed suit: in December, New Hampshire militia took Fort William and Mary, in Portsmouth, removing cannon and ammunition, while the Rhode Island militia stole 44 guns from Fort George, in Newport.

Meanwhile, the routine of garrison life – desertion, drunkenness and street fights – continued through the winter of 1774. With both polluted water supplies (caused by the exceptionally mild winter weather) and poor

*Gage's deputy, General Haldimand, estimated that the Provincial Congress could mobilise 30,000 men without harming the economy of Massachusetts.

BOSTON HARBOUR AND SURROUNDING ISLANDS

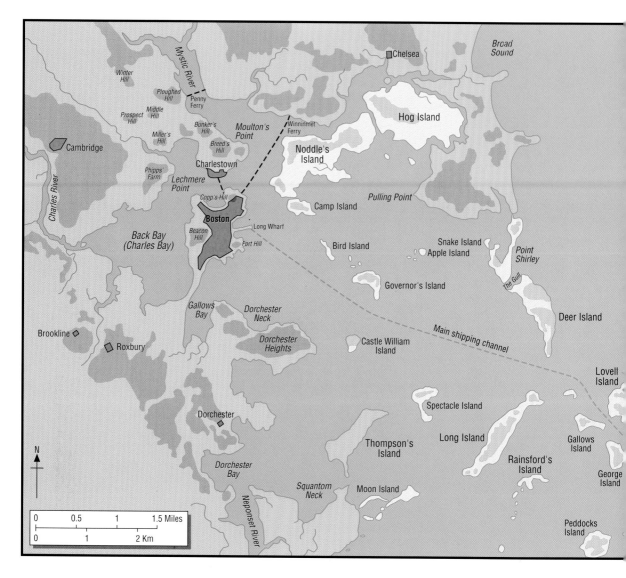

quarters contributing to a death-toll of over 100 among the garrison and its dependants, Gage's continued attempts to placate the towns-people further alienated his troops, and encouraged insulting editorials in Whig newspapers. He tried to keep the troops out of trouble by sending them on marches into the countryside, but while alarming the populace, he also provided the militia with an opportunity to perfect their 'early warning' system. Within hours of an alarm, up to 12,000 irregulars could be mobilised and marching to intercept the regulars.

On 26 February 1774, Lieutenant Colonel Alexander Leslie took the 64th from Castle William to seize the cannon being stored near Salem, in Essex County. However, he was met by Colonel Thomas Pickering and his Essex

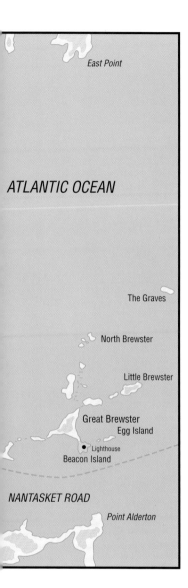

East Point

ATLANTIC OCEAN

The Graves

North Brewster

Little Brewster

Great Brewster
Egg Island
Lighthouse
Beacon Island

NANTASKET ROAD

Point Alderton

William Legge, 2nd Earl of Dartmouth (1731-1801), was step-brother of Lord North. He became Secretary of State for the Colonies in 1772 and was known as a friend of the colonists, despite his strong views on the supremacy of Parliament. A gentle, pious man (associated with the early Methodists), he was succeeded as Secretary of State by Lord George Germain in November 1775. (National Portrait Gallery, London)

Paul Revere (1735-1818) was leader of the Boston 'mechanics' (skilled labourers), and an effective political cartoonist. He was a trusted messenger of the Committee of Safety, as well as being a silversmith. He had served at Crown Point in 1756 and took part in the Boston Tea Party. He remained largely unknown until the 1860s when an inaccurate, romanticised, account of his 'ride' conveniently ignored his capture, and the efforts of Dawes and Dr Prescott. (Museum of Fine Arts, Boston)

militia, and though the accounts of each side differ, the upshot was that the guns were spirited away and Leslie was forced to return empty-handed.

Until now, the marches had involved individual regiments, but on 30 March, Lord Percy led his entire brigade – over 1200 men – to Jamaica Plain, five miles south of Boston. He met the usual hostility from the inhabitants, but also found that the militia had both dismantled the only bridge into Cambridge over the Charles River, and set up two cannon to guard the bridge at Watertown. On each occasion, he turned away, an act the militia saw as a sign that any resolute stand by them would force the regulars to withdraw. Despite both sides' strict orders not to fire unless fired upon, it was only a matter of time before such confrontations led to bloodshed.

In April, Gage received a message from Lord Dartmouth, Secretary of State for the American Colonies, authorising stronger action – if war was inevitable, better it should start now, before the Americans were prepared. That January, Gage had called for officers to survey and map the countryside. Captain Brown (52nd Foot) and Ensign de Berniere (10th Foot) had responded and explored Worcester and Suffolk counties, avoiding capture by sheer good fortune (and a snowstorm). They reported that the countryside favoured the Americans and any expedition could only end in disaster.

On 20 March Gage ordered them to reconnoitre the roads in Middlesex County, where they duly discovered military stores at Concord in the course of their mission.

Informed by Dr Church that the Provincial Congress would soon adjourn, with the delegates dispersing to the four corners of Massachusetts, Gage decided to act. On Saturday 15 April he ordered the flank companies to be taken off normal duties and asked the Royal Navy commander, Vice-Admiral Samuel Graves to prepare the boats from his ships. Paul Revere, a Boston silversmith, reported these activities to Dr Joseph Warren of the Committee of Safety, who arranged for four 6-pdr guns to be removed from Concord. Revere then rode to Lexington to inform Hancock and Adams that they might also be the British objective.

THE OPPOSING COMMANDERS

THE BRITISH COMMANDERS

Throughout the war, British (and most American) officers were 'gentlemen'. However undemocratic this appears today, without formal military colleges it made sense – they were better educated, used to giving orders and (mostly) accepted the notion of *noblesse oblige* (power creating responsibility). Their lifestyles allowed them to maintain a military hierarchy, while retaining social equality and brotherly familiarity, and hunting gave them some experience in fieldcraft and handling weapons (especially firearms, which were very expensive).

Lieutenant General the Hon Thomas Gage (1719-1787), was commander-in-chief in North America after 1763 and also Governor of Massachusetts after April 1774. A soldier from his teens, he had served at Fontenoy, Culloden, Monongahela, Ticonderoga and in Amherst's campaigns, for which he had formed the first British unit of light-armed infantry (though taking little further interest beyond the benefits of his 'colonelcy'). Despite frequent rumours of 'shyness' in the face of the enemy, there is no evidence to suggest that his lacklustre command performances were caused by anything more than well-intentioned caution. Recalled in September 1775, he found himself out of favour and stripped of his offices, and had to wait for a change of government before becoming a General in 1782.

Gage's Royal Navy counterpart was Samuel Graves (1713-1787), Vice Admiral of the Blue, and commander of the American squadron from July 1774, whose area of responsibility stretched from Canada to the Caribbean. Graves joined the Navy in 1739 and served at Cartagena and Quiberon Bay, before becoming a Rear Admiral in 1772. Despite his own problems with inadequate ships and crews, he tried to help Gage wherever possible, advocating an aggressive stance. Unpopular with the Army, and wrongly blamed for the failure of combined operations on 17 June 1775, and later, he was sent home in January and replaced by Richard Howe, but became an Admiral in 1778.

Major General William Howe (1729-1814) had been a brother officer of James Wolfe in the 20th Foot, and had, over the years, both successfully

LEFT *This famous painting by Joshua Reynolds shows Major General John Burgoyne (1722-1792) at his most dashing, in the uniform of a colonel of a light dragoon regiment. Away from Army life, Burgoyne was an MP and wrote successful, if somewhat tedious, plays (including a farce, 'The Siege of Boston', which was interrupted by the raid on Charlestown). A mild Tory, he was also fond of political intrigue and criticised Gage, Howe and Clinton in succession. (The Frick Collection, New York)*

ABOVE *At 37 Major General Henry Clinton (1738–1795) was the youngest of the three generals to arrive aboard the* Cerberus, *and the only one to write an account – largely self-justifying, it must be said – of his American campaigns. Apart from Washington, no other officer on either side held a senior command longer. (National Army Museum, London)*

trained and commanded light infantry units serving at Quebec, Montreal, Belle Isle and Havana (where he was Adjutant General). In 1772 he was made a Major General, and two years later was chosen to promote a new light infantry drill. Though he led bravely on 17 June, he lost sight of his greater responsibilities and behaved too much like a regimental officer. He took over command from Gage, receiving the 'local' rank of General in October 1775 and was commander-in-chief until recalled in 1778 to answer charges that he and his brother Richard had prolonged the war for their own gain, though he later held large home commands during the Napoleonic Wars.

Major General Henry Clinton (1738-1795) was a former New York militia officer, and the only son of Admiral George Clinton, a past governor of that colony. A short, plump, unimposing man who had served in Germany during the Seven Years War (leading him to undervalue officers with American experience), he displayed great bravery and tactical skill on 17 June. His failing, particularly evident after his wife's death, was extreme sensitivity to the point of paranoia. After the evacuation, he was Howe's deputy and succeeded him as commander-in-chief.

Hugh, Lord Percy (1742-1817) was Colonel of the 5th Foot, and showed himself to be a generous and progressive officer, instituting good conduct and long service awards, as well as providing funds and transport home for the regiment's widows after 17 June. In those days, there was nothing unusual in social fraternisation between political, or even military, opponents, and he was popular with many Americans, often being entertained at the Hancock house on Boston Common. (The Percy family and Fusiliers Museum of Northumberland)

Major General John Burgoyne (1722-1792) was the oldest, but most junior, of the three British Army Commanders, having seen no action until he was 36. A cavalry officer, he soon rose to prominence through genuine ability, allied with the influence of his father-in-law, the Earl of Derby, after serving at St Malo and Cherbourg. He established the first light horse units in the Army, and in 1762 carried out a daring raid in Portugal (Charles Lee was a subordinate). A gallant soldier, but described by a colleague as 'vain boastful and superficial, and not a man to depend on in a tight corner', he remained in Boston on 17 June, but recorded what he saw of the battle. His humane treatment of the rank and file earned him the nickname 'Gentleman Johnny' and, for all his faults, his treatise for officers on leading their men was ahead of its time. Condemned for his failure at Saratoga, he was briefly commander-in-chief in Ireland, before being ousted by political opponents.

Brigadier General Hugh, Lord Percy (1742-1817) had joined the Army at 17 and progressed rapidly (by purchase) from Ensign to Lieutenant Colonel in three years. Quiet and unostentatious, he was a distinguished veteran of the Seven Years War, and served in the Guards before becoming the King's aide-de-camp. Despite his pro-Whig views, he volunteered to serve in America in 1774, and showed skill and coolness in saving Smith's column on 19 April. He returned home in 1777 as a Lieutenant General, but held no further military command; he succeeded as Duke of Northumberland in 1786.

Brigadier General Robert Pigott (or Pigot) (1720-1796) was famous for his lack of inches, but compensated for this with an aggressiveness and bravery noted by Howe during the attack on Breed's Hill. From a military family, one brother, Lord George Pigott, became Governor of Madras in 1775, and another, Hugh, was an Admiral.

Lieutenant Colonel Francis Smith (1723-1791) joined the 10th Foot as a Captain in 1747 and became its Lieutenant Colonel in 1762. In 1767 it went to America, but he may have preceded this move as he is credited with 12 years' service there by September 1775. Wounded on 19 April that same year, he asked to retire in August, but was persuaded to remain and breveted Colonel in September. Despite another inauspicious performance at Dorchester Heights in March 1776, he led a brigade at New York and Newport (Rhode Island), before returning to England to become a Major General in 1779 and a Lieutenant General in 1787.

Major John Pitcairn (1722-1775) was commissioned Captain in the Marines in 1756 and promoted major on 19 April 1771. A Scot with 11 children, he commanded the first Marines sent to Boston, turning a collection of detachments into a first-class unit (he even lived in the barracks with his men to stop them buying alcohol). Described as 'perhaps the only British officer. . . who commanded the trust and liking of the inhabitants', he played a prominent role on 19 April 1775, and was mortally wounded on Breed's Hill, falling into the arms of his son, and adjutant, Thomas. His loss was felt deeply by his men.

Two other officers bear mentioning — Lieutenant Colonel Samuel Cleveland, who commanded Gage's artillery, and Captain John Montresor, the senior (and only) engineer. Cleveland apparently spent his time chasing a local teacher's daughters, and seems to have been responsible (despite his protestations) for Percy's guns running out of ammunition at Lexington, as well as the ammunition debacle on Breed's Hill. The almost permanent absence of two company commanders on leave also suggests a certain lack of control on his behalf.

Captain Montresor had followed in the footsteps of his famous father, Lieutenant Colonel James Montresor (also an engineer), but despite extensive American service – including combat experience – both a lack of formal training and his possession of a somewhat paranoid personality led to his talents being under-utilised. He designed Boston's defences competently enough, and mapped some of the surrounding area, but failed to survey Charlestown peninsula, although Gage may share some responsibility for this lapse.

THE AMERICAN COMMANDERS

Before dealing with the better-known American leaders, it is useful to look at one who led only a detachment and who, if not typical in terms of background, certainly typified the spirit of the militia's company officers. Captain John Parker, who commanded at Lexington, was 45 years old and, as a veteran of Rogers' Rangers, had been an obvious choice as a leader of a company of 'minute men'. A mature and sensible farmer who was married with seven children, his actions on 19 April 1775 are at variance with his known experience and military abilities, and suggest that he was acting under orders (probably from Samuel Adams) in lining up his men (who were also his friends and neighbours) in a suicidal, and militarily useless, position that morning.

General George Washington (1732-1799) had already undertaken several dangerous military missions before being appointed Lieutenant Colonel of the Virginia militia. His various independent commands enjoyed mixed fortunes, but he served bravely as aide-de-camp to Braddock in the Monongahela campaign, before resigning his commission in 1759. A prominent opponent of British policy, he was a delegate at the first Continental Congress, but his appointment as commander-in-chief in 1775 was a political 'fix' to encourage southern involvement in the war. He took command on 3 July 1775, and although his military decisions during the siege were few, he had nevertheless to organise an ad hoc collection of men from several colonies into an army, while coping with constant changes in personnel as enlistment periods expired. Militarily, he was a poor tactician who, in seven years, won no major battles and suffered unnecessary defeats. He resigned as commander-in-chief in 1783, but was reinstated in 1798 when war with France seemed likely.

Major General Artemas Ward (1727-1800), was of pilgrim-Massachusetts stock. Honest, hard working and efficient, he had held public office before becoming Brigadier General and second-in-command of the Massachusetts militia in 1774. On 20 April 1775 he took command at Boston, and directed operations on 17 June, recognising better than most the virtues and limitations of his men. He became the senior Major General of the Continental Army, retaining *de facto* command until Washington's arrival,

ABOVE *An undistinguished officer, Lieutenant Colonel Francis Smith's (1723-1791) command of the Concord expedition was probably based either on his seniority in the garrison, or his long-term friendship with Gage (whose experience of service in America, and views on dealing with civilians and private property, he shared). Even in this painting, executed around the time of the Seven Years War, judging by the uniform, he is overweight; in spite of consistently poor performances, he rose to high rank, though only in home commands. (National Army Museum, London)*

RIGHT *For a man who had no formal education after the age of 15 (and remained deficient in all but mathematics throughout his life), General George Washington (1732-1799) was an impressive leader, possessing height, bearing, composure and unfailing dignity and courtesy. He is shown here in typically 'heroic' pose, supervising the emplacement of Knox's guns on Dorchester Heights, with Boston and its harbour visible in the background.*

Major General Artemas Ward (1727-1800) was of heavy build and medium height, with a slow speech and stern countenance. His long militia service, including action at Ticonderoga, had permanently damaged his health and he was often required to rise from his sick bed during the first months of the campaign. Despite his qualities, he was rejected for further command by both Washington and Massachusetts. (Independence National Historical Park, Philadelphia)

At the council of war on 16 June, General Israel Putnam (1718-1790) reputedly offered the sage advice: 'Americans are not at all afraid of their heads, though very much afraid of their legs; if you cover these, they will fight for ever.' A wealthy man, following a successful marriage and land speculation along the Mississippi, he narrowly escaped execution by Indians during the colonial wars, but most stories about him, though entertaining, are apocryphal. (Anne S K Brown Military Collection, Brown University Library)

but never hid his disappointment at being superseded, and the latter's views on the state and discipline of his army upset him. After the British withdrawal, he became commander of the Eastern Department until replaced by William Heath in March 1777.

Major General William Heath (1737-1814) was a fifth generation Massachusetts American, a farmer, a militia officer and a politician. Of middling stature and light complexion, corpulent and bald, he had never seen action, but read military literature and belonged to Boston's Ancient and Honourable Artillery Company. Appointed brigadier general by the Provincial Congress in February 1775, he was the senior officer present on 19 April, and made the original dispositions for the siege, but did little thereafter, confirming Washington's view of him as over-cautious. He replaced Ward in command of the Eastern Department and supervised Rochambeau's reception in 1780. At the time of his death, he was the last surviving major general of the Revolution.

General Israel Putnam (1718-1790) was a New England legend before the Revolution. Standing 5ft 6in tall, and powerfully built, he joined Rogers'

Rangers during the French and Indian Wars, commanded a provincial regiment under Amherst, was shipwrecked on the Havana expedition and fought in Pontiac's War. He took command of the 3rd Connecticut regiment in May 1775, becoming a Brigadier General of the Connecticut troops in June. Worshipped by his soldiers and considered a 'good Colonel' by brother officers, 'Old Put' was, however, no field commander, and he was later relegated to organising recruits. He retired in 1779 following a stroke.

Colonel William Prescott (1726-1795), a veteran of two colonial wars, was a prosperous Massachusetts farmer and played a leading role in the council of war on 16 June 1775. Over 6ft tall, well-built and noted for his coolness under pressure, he was an inspiring leader, and one of the few officers the militia would unhesitatingly obey. Despite the debate over whether he or Putnam commanded on 17 June, it was undoubtedly Prescott who led the defenders on Breed's Hill. He later became Colonel of a Continental regiment, before age and an old farming injury led him to retire in 1777.

Colonel John Stark (1728-1822) was a Scots-Irish former Captain in Rogers' Rangers. Of medium height, with bold features and piercing blue eyes, he was the stuff of frontier legends, fully understanding battlefield psychology, but was an insubordinate and cussed individual. In April 1775 he became Colonel of the 1st New Hampshire regiment (in which his son Caleb was an Ensign) and commanded the left flank on 17 June. He served through the war, reaching the rank of Major General.

Colonel James Reed (1723-1807) was poorly educated, but had served as a Captain at Ticonderoga and Crown Point. In April 1775, he was appointed Colonel of the 3rd New Hampshire regiment and defended the rail fence on 17 June. He went on to command a brigade in 1776, but resigned when illness left him blind and partially deaf.

Colonel Richard Gridley (1710-1796) was a fourth generation Bostonian, and a surveyor and civil engineer who had served in the French and Indian Wars, and had built several forts before retiring on half pay. In 1775, he became chief engineer and colonel of the Massachusetts artillery regiment, apparently striking a hard financial bargain with the Provincial Congress and promoting two sons to commands in the regiment. He was wounded on 17 June, and replaced as chief of the Continental Artillery by Knox due to age. He was not well thought of by many (including Washington), but does seem to have done good work during the siege.

Noted for his bravery and leadership, Captain Thomas Knowlton (1740-1776) joined the militia at 15, was a Lieutenant during the French and Indian Wars and served at Havana in 1762. Lean and over 6ft tall, he led part of Putnam's regiment, and on 17 June protected Prescott's left flank with Stark and Reed. Promoted to Major, he led a successful raid on Charlestown in January 1776, but was killed later that year at Harlem Heights.

Dr Joseph Warren (1741-1775) graduated in medicine from Harvard in 1759 and was a successful Boston doctor. An associate of Adams and Hancock (he eventually replaced the latter as president of the Provincial Congress), he gave the oration on the first two anniversaries of the 'Boston Massacre', drafted the 'Suffolk Resolves' and organised the alarm riders. Dr

Dr Joseph Warren (1741-1775) was the distinguished political orator and author of the 'Suffolk Resolves', which attacked the Intolerable Acts. He was also popular for providing medical treatment to rich and poor alike. Killed instantly on 17 June (making none of the famous pre-death speeches ascribed to him), he was buried in an unmarked grave on Breed's Hill and became one of the first corpses to be identified by dental records – two false teeth made by Paul Revere. (Independence National Historical Park, Philadelphia)

Warren was present on 19 April, later being appointed Major General, and served as a volunteer on 17 June, before being killed at the fall of the redoubt.

Brigadier General Seth Pomeroy (1706-1777), a prominent and prosperous Massachusetts gunsmith, was a veteran of the French and Indian Wars. Tall, lean and intrepid, he was a delegate at the first two Provincial Congresses, and became Brigadier General of the militia in October 1774. Like Warren, he served as a volunteer on 17 June, but survived the battle to be appointed Major General of the Massachusetts militia on 20 June. He declined an appointment from Congress and spent the rest of his life training and drilling recruits.

Other senior officers who held commands during the siege, but played little part in it, included Major General Charles Lee (1731-1782), third in command after Washington and Ward, and Brigadier General Horatio Gates (1728-1806), Washington's Adjutant General (both former British officers with American experience); and Brigadier Generals Nathanael Greene (1742-1786), commanding the Rhode Island contingent, Joseph Spencer (1714-1789), a veteran of the French and Indian Wars and commander of the Connecticut contingent, and John Sullivan (1740-1795), the senior New Hampshire officer, and leader of the force which successfully captured Fort William and Mary.

THE OPPOSING ARMIES

THE BRITISH ARMY AND THE ROYAL NAVY

In 1775, the British Army, as a royal institution, was 115 years old (a few regiments did, however, predate this) and comprised two Establishments, British and Irish, paid for by their respective governments – the attempt to create a third in North America was one cause of the Revolution. On paper, its strength was 48,647 men, but actual numbers were far less – for example, the 13,500-strong Irish Establishment (which provided most of the Boston units) had just 7000 under arms, and of 8600 men notionally in America, only 7000 existed, with further absences leaving the total of soldiers present and fit for duty nearer the 5000 mark.

These shortfalls were principally due to the soldiers' poor treatment and equally poor public image, which made recruitment almost impossible, and encouraged desertion. Taxpaying voters in Britain saw a peacetime army as an extravagance and a threat to liberty, and such characteristically Anglo-Saxon views naturally found their way to North America – only in Scotland was soldiering an honourable occupation.

'Six pence a day' – this satirical cartoon makes the point that even juvenile chimney sweeps could earn twice as much as a soldier. Yet, though the soldier's lot was undoubtedly not a happy one, unlike most civilians, he did not have to look for accommodation or food – and, for what it was worth, he had a job for life, since poor recruitment encouraged the Army to retain men for as long as they could stand. (Anne S K Brown Military Collection, Brown University Library)

THE BRITISH ARMY
AND ROYAL NAVY

CANADA 7th, 26th Foot

UPPER LAKES 8th Foot

ILLINOIS 18th Foot (2 Cos)

HALIFAX 65th Foot (8 Cos)

VIRGINIA 14th Foot

NEW YORK 18th Foot (5 Cos)

FLORIDA 16th Foot

BOSTON (I Bgde) 4th, 23rd, 47th Foot
(II Bgde) 5th, 38th, 52nd Foot
(III Bgde) 10th, 18th/65th (5 Cos[1]),
43rd, 59th Foot
(Unbrigaded) 1st Marines
Castle William: 64th Foot
Artillery: 4th Bn, RA (5 Cos)

Notes:
1. Because of their low strength, the companies of the
   18th and 65th Foot formed an 'Incorporated
   Corps'.

ROYAL NAVY: NORTH AMERICAN SQUADRON, 1 JANUARY 1775[1]

VESSEL	GUNS	VESSEL	GUNS
Asia	70	Canceaux	8[3]
Boyne	64	Cruizer	8
Somerset	64	Savage	8
Preston	50	Diana	6
Tartar	28	Diligent	6
Fowey	20[2]	Gaspee	6[4]
Glasgow	20	Halifax	6
Lively	20	Hope	6
Mercury	20	Magdalan	6
Rose	20	St John	6
Scarborough	20		
Kingfisher	16		
Swan	16		
Tamer	16		

Notes:
1. Graves had a total of 24 ships, which would rise to
   29 by mid-June with the arrival of the 14-gun
   sloops *Falcon, Merlin, Nautilus, Otter* and *Senegal.*
2. Main armament for 20-, 16- and 14-gun ships was
   9-pdrs.
3. Main armament for 8- and 6-gun vessels was
   6-pdrs.
4. Not the same ship as that burnt in June 1772.

In America, vast distances exacerbated the problem of replacements, and departing units usually 'drafted' their own men back to the incoming regiment, while the officers, NCOs and staff returned home to recruit. Garrison life in the western forts was better than the norm (the Indians and the size of the country made life slightly more dangerous, but discouraged desertion), and only in towns and ports, where they were 'quartered' with the civilian population, did desertion, disorder and drunkenness return. Barracks were disliked in England because they made a *coup d'état* easier to organise, as well as costing money to build. In America they were particularly despised because they implied a permanent military presence.

Revolutionary folklore depicts the British soldier as a criminal and illiterate drunkard – doubtless some individuals were bad (others inevitably became so in boring, hostile garrisons like Boston), but most were ordinary men, often skilled, sometimes literate, who joined primarily to avoid unemployment. Though lacking the individual skills of their citizen-soldier opponents, they were better trained – lapses in discipline during the campaign owed more to the frustrations of garrison duty than any fundamental flaws in the regimental system – and they showed exceptional stamina and determination on 19 April. When their pride was affronted, as on 17 June, *esprit de corps* and dogged bravery would make up for any other failings.

The stereotypical officer – lazy, amateurish and decadent – was also rare in America; he would have rather resigned, or exchanged regiments, than serve in such a social backwater. A long peace inevitably led to stagnation and an element of 'dead wood', but this disappeared surprisingly quickly on active service. The majority could be as professional as their

The rifles carried by some units, such as the 1st Pennsylvania Rifles shown here, were more accurate than the smoothbore musket but were slower to load and lacked a bayonet. (Michael Roffe)

French or Prussian counterparts, lacking nothing in courage, and invariably winning the confidence of their men through fair treatment and shared hardships. Combined with a core of professional NCOs, they provided effective battlefield leadership – ironically, the low leader-to-men ratio resulting from manpower shortages undoubtedly made this easier.

THE INFANTRY

The infantry comprised regiments of foot, numbered in order of seniority, whose principal tactical formations were the battalion and the platoon (synonymous, in peacetime, with the administrative units of the regiment and company). Battalions had a nominal establishment of 477 officers and men in ten companies – eight 'centre' companies (from their position in the line on parade or in battle), and two 'flank' companies (grenadiers and light infantry, or 'picquets'). Companies usually had a captain, lieutenant and ensign, with two sergeants, three corporals, a drummer and 38 privates, though only 'flank' companies were kept near full strength, usually by plundering the centre companies' best men. Regimental staff included the colonel, lieutenant colonel and major, a chaplain, adjutant (usually a company officer), surgeon and surgeon's mate, and a pioneer squad.

As there was no standard drill-book until the 1790s, chaos often reigned in this crucial area of military life within the British Army, although most officers read certain standard texts, such as the 1764 *Manual Exercise*. The standard formation was three ranks – two if manpower was short – and firing and manoeuvring were by 'platoons' (equivalent to a company, but often under different officers, creating further confusion). Peacetime parsimony limited 'live firing', but the regulars' platoon fire could still be a potent moral and physical weapon, though inexperience seems to have led many of the Boston units to fire too high in action.

As was customary, the grenadier and light companies were detached to form 'converged' battalions, a practice that gave a commander an elite advance guard and reserve, but stripped the battalions of their best subunits. Such battalions also needed time to acquire *esprit de corps*, as the men got used to strange officers (Gage may have chosen the flank companies for the Concord raid to speed up this process) and, as the campaign showed, their role almost guaranteed heavy losses that were only replaceable by compulsory 'recruitment' from parent units (or amalgamation, as with the 18th's and 65th's grenadiers).

THE MARINES

The Marines (they only became 'Royal' in 1802) were the Royal Navy's private army, administered by the Admiralty and controlled by senior naval officers. The rank-and-file were volunteers and wore Army-style uniforms and equipment. However they were trained to serve on warships and undertake amphibious operations. In addition long periods of sea service encouraged personal marksmanship and initiative (sergeants often commanded a ship's contingent). The 50 companies, shared between Chatham, Portsmouth and Plymouth, were not regimented, and detachments, or in

A Private of the Light Company of the 38th foot which was stationed in Boston in 1775 and fought at Lexington and Breed's Hill. (Gerry Embleton)

some cases individual replacements, were assigned on an *ad hoc* basis.

The first Marines sent to Boston were to form a battalion of 600 men under Major Pitcairn, but by 12 March only 336 were present, and they soon became an object of inter-service rivalry over pay, food and conditions as Graves tried (in vain) to retain the best men. Although initially physically inferior to their Army comrades, and short of essential equipment for service on land, incessant drilling and regular marches into the countryside soon created a fine unit. Another group (41 officers, 53 NCOs, 20 drummers and over 600 other ranks, many of whom had asked to serve in America) arrived in May, and the whole force formed two battalions, with grenadier and light companies.

THE CAVALRY

The only cavalry unit in Boston was the 17th Light Dragoons, which arrived from Ireland in June 1775. Peacetime establishment was 231 all ranks, in six troops, which was increased to 288 in April, but as the 17th sailed from Cork that very month, they may not have adopted this organisational structure. The staff comprised a lieutenant colonel, major, chaplain, adjutant and surgeon, plus various craftsmen to tend the horses. Each troop had a captain, lieutenant, cornet and sergeant, two corporals, a musician and 37 privates. A new wartime establishment added 34 officers and men per troop, but a lesser number of horses, leading to the formation of 'dismounted divisions' for American service (the 17th did not receive these while in Boston).

Light dragoons originated as light troops of dragoon regiments around 1759 (equivalent to the infantry's 'picquets'). Their special duties – outpost work, reconnaissance, escorts and messengers – involved greater individual responsibility. Consequently, the men were better treated and regarded themselves as an elite. A small detachment apparently accompanied Howe on 17 June, but their most famous action was to 'convert' the Old South meeting house into a riding school, officers' club and piggery!

THE ARTILLERY

The Royal Regiment of Artillery emerged from the Seven Years War with a reputation for innovation, aggression and competence – but peace had blunted these qualities and their overall performance in the campaign was lacklustre (possibly due more to the shortcomings of the commander than of the men). Unlike the other arms, the artillery was controlled by the Board of Ordnance, and made its own arrangements for almost everything, even specialised naval transport.

There were 48 companies in four battalions – those in Boston were all from the 4th Battalion, raised in 1771 and never before used in action. Companies contained only personnel – a captain, six other officers (including three lieutenant-fireworkers), three sergeants, three corporals, 20 gunners, 62 matrosses and two drummers – with guns and vehicles allocated according to the task in hand (for example, a detachment under Lieutenant Colonel Thomas James manned the guns on the 'gondolas', which were flatboats with a 12-pdr cannon at each end, protected by planking along the sides). Although the practice had been dying out, the campaign saw lighter pieces (6-pdrs) used as battalion guns for infantry support, whilst the heavier guns (12-pdrs) formed separate units.

THE ROYAL NAVY

The Royal Navy had not yet become the all-powerful force it would be in the Napoleonic Wars. Controlled by the Admiralty in London, it protected British colonies and maintained vital trade links, and unlike the Army, it was therefore popular with the public – except in ports, where the 'press gangs' operated ruthlessly.

Graves' squadron had to prevent smuggling, contraband trade, arms smuggling and the rising incidence of attacks on Loyalists and royal officials, from Nova Scotia to the Floridas, as well as providing crews for the Army's fleet of small craft, including the gondolas (which forced Graves to strip the crews of his own ships). To achieve all this, Graves had a makeshift assortment of ships, mostly in bad condition and needing urgent refits, many of which had crews below even peacetime strength – manpower was a constant problem and Graves was frequently in trouble with civil authorities for 'pressing' civilians. His ships were all of the wrong types – the *Asia*, *Boyne* and *Somerset* were too big to get into the shallows and bombard the shore, while the sloops and brigs were out-gunned by the big American privateers preying on Gage's defenceless transports and supply vessels.

Hostility in Boston resulted in a constant shortage of stores, and the nearest naval base was 500 miles away in Halifax. Finally, there was a shortage of ships' boats – especially flat-bottomed troop carriers – which did all the hard work around the harbour, ferried personnel around the defences, and mounted vital patrols at night. Despite all this, the Royal Navy did its best, and helped Gage out of several scrapes.

THE AMERICAN FORCES

There can have been few campaigns where one side has successfully disbanded and totally recreated its military organisation within sight and sound of the enemy, without suffering catastrophic defeat; the Americans did this three times during the Boston campaign. In October 1774 they began reorganising the militia to be able to oppose any force Gage might send against it (which it duly did, successfully, on 19 April). Then, inside two months, they formed the army which besieged Boston and fought on 17 June. Their final creation was a national force, to take over after the expiry of the enlistment periods of the former army on 31 December 1775, and which brought America that much nearer its first permanent standing army.

The rhetoric of colonial opposition had denied the need for a standing army in America – enthusiastic militia (free of the stigma of the King's 'paid hirelings') were enough, as the events of 19 April 1775 seemed to prove.

However, idealism obscured the faults of the Provincial system and handicapped the American war effort until Congress finally grasped the nettle to create an American 'New Model' army. In the meantime, the need to appease varying political views would prevent Washington from imposing military solutions for military problems.

THE MASSACHUSETTS MILITIA

The colonies had always had a militia based on English lines – indeed, the Massachusetts militia predated the British Army by almost 40 years – but its subsequent evolution was the result of purely local needs. As the colonies expanded, defence began further from home and long absences caused economic problems, so units of volunteers, or 'drafts', garrisoned remote outposts and made long-range raids. By the 1750s, the famous 'rangers' and other 'provincial' regiments, had evolved, but far from improving the militia, these 'quasi-regular' units made the existence of local defensive forces appear pointless. As danger became more remote, musters became social events (as they had in England), and some Colonies used Provincials (and even regulars) as an excuse to do nothing to defend themselves. The poor performance of some provincial regiments, and the militia's clumsy drill routines, especially after a Sunday morning's drinking, merely confirmed the already poor view some British officers had of the inhabitants' fighting abilities.

Following Gage's surprise raid on Charlestown, Worcester reorganised its militia and the new system was quickly adopted throughout New England. A quarter of the men were formed into companies of 'minute men' (ready for action at a moment's notice) who received the best equipment and were composed of the best men. In contrast to British regiments, where 'drafting' was a chance to 'lose' bad or sick men, the militia seems to have parted willingly with its finest. Nine such companies formed a regiment, with the men electing a captain and two lieutenants who, in turn, elected the regimental staff and commanding officer. The dispersed nature of the population meant that company strengths and catchment areas varied, so sub-units were more widely used and had more tactical value than in the British Army.

By April 1775, the 'minute men' – and the militia generally – were by no means as inferior to the regulars as is often stated, and though older, had more combat veterans (possibly one man in three), especially among the company officers, where the British had none.

Nor was the 'minute men' idea new – variations on the theme had been seen in colonial wars back to the 1650s, and the challenge of recreating their own elite force, along with the concentration of experienced men and

This Ensign of the 55th Foot is carrying the Regimental Colour which with the King's Colourserved as a rallying-point and station-keeping device. This regiment, later to become the 2nd Bn., the Border Regiment, arrived in Boston in December 1775. (Gerry Embleton)

Timothy Pickering (1745-1829) was a serious military student and colonel of the Essex militia, whose Easy Plan of Discipline for a Militia (based on the English Norfolk Discipline) was used by all Massachusetts troops until superceded by von Steuben's regulations. Despite confronting Leslie at Salem, he was reluctant to intercept Percy's column near Charlestown on 19 April, and went home the next day in protest at the bellicose nature of many of the militia. (Independence National Historical Park, Philadelphia)

the replacement of Tory sympathisers among senior regimental officers, boosted the militia's confidence in its ability to face the regulars in action.

Using tactics ideally suited to their typically individual, rather than collective, martial skills, allowed the 'minute men', ordinary militia and 'alarm' companies (the few remaining men too young, old or unfit to serve elsewhere) to harass Smith's column from Concord back to Boston. It was only the lack of experienced commanders and a tried and tested chain of command above company level that prevented the destruction of the regulars; this failing also allowed the British to inflict losses on the militia by making it impossible to co-ordinate a response to their use of outflanking tactics. By 20 April, Boston was surrounded by 441 companies of militia, but lack of discipline and centralised control made this force incapable of offensive operations.

THE ARMY OF OBSERVATION

The Committee of Safety proposed an army of 30,000 New Englanders, including 13,600 from Massachusetts, in one artillery and 23 infantry regiments. An infantry regiment had ten companies, each with a captain, two lieutenants, four sergeants, four corporals, a drummer, a fifer and 66 privates (reduced to 46 to retain as many officers as possible). The colonel (who could also be a general) lieutenant colonel and major doubled as captains, as in the British Army, and there were six regimental staff, plus an extra major for regiments commanded by a general. The men were selected after inspections in the lines, rather than by town quotas traditionally used to raise provincial units.

The other New England provincial congresses responded to the news of Lexington. Many individuals arrived from New Hampshire, still a 'frontier' colony and boasting many Rogers' Rangers veterans, and formed two *ad hoc* units under Stark and Sargent. A quota of 1900 men in three regiments, was agreed, and their ten-company organisation differed only in having 53 privates per company and eight regimental staff.

Rhode Island authorised 1500 men in three regiments (two with eight companies, one with seven plus an artillery company), and offered Providence County's militia brigade until they were ready. Regiments had seven staff and companies comprised three officers, six NCOs, two musicians and 49 privates (two extra companies were later added to each regiment). The best equipped and organised New England force, it was extremely egalitarian, with no seniority among the officers, or the regiments (which had no numbers and occupied 'posts of honour' by rota).

The Connecticut militia mobilised immediately, but were ordered to wait until the assembly met. It authorised 6000 men in six regiments, and companies were drawn from towns on a proportional basis. The regiments were large with companies of four officers and 100 enlisted men (the number of privates was later reduced from 90 to 65), and upheld the British custom of generals also being colonels, and field officers captains, though the extra officer in each company made this less burdensome.

The army showed considerable commonality amongst individual militia forces – hardly surprising with their history of military co-operation. There were delays in mobilising, but those affected probably benefitted – Massachusetts' hasty efforts were chaotic, with the Provincial Congress and Committee of Safety often at cross-purposes. For all units, however, arms and ammunition were scarce, limiting operational capabilities just as much as the lack of centralised command structure. The councils of war merely decided by consensus, preventing effective planning and obscuring the army's real needs, as would be seen on 17 June.

THE CONTINENTAL ARMY

The Second Continental Congress was persuaded by the New England delegation to adopt their army as a national one, which it did on 14 June 1775, ordering 10,000 (later raised to 22,000) men for Boston. It also authorised a rifle regiment of ten companies – six (later nine) plus the regimental staff from Pennsylvania, and two each from Maryland and Virginia – each consisting of five officers, four sergeants, a hornist and 72 rank-and-file, enlisting for one year. The regiment arrived in Boston in July, where its frontier habits and general cussedness made it a disciplinary nightmare.

Congress also made administrative appointments – adjutant, quartermaster, paymaster and commissary generals – as well as four major generals and eight brigadier generals, based on the numbers of men from each colony. Washington used them to form divisions and brigades along British lines, and adopted British systems for logistical and supply organisations (by contrast, the artillery remained part of the army and applicants for medical posts were carefully scrutinised).

On taking command, Washington noted the inherent problems in the Main Army (so-called to distinguish it from the Separate Army invading Canada), including differing regimental structures, the weakness of many Massachusetts regiments and the incompetence of some officers due to the method of their selection. Reforms were approved by Congress, but with only weeks until the entire army's enlistment period expired, such radical reorganisation was best left to the new year.

The 'Continental' regiments would have eight companies (considered more manoeuvrable than ten), each of four officers, four sergeants, four corporals, two musicians and 76 privates, sub-divided into four squads. With 88 per cent of the unit musket-armed (and operating in two ranks, not three), firepower was maximised, while the squad system, and a one-to-ten leader/men ratio, improved tactical flexibility in what was extremely difficult terrain.

By November, enough officers had re-enlisted to command the 26 regiments, and there was even a surplus of captains. Washington chose the new colonels who, with their brigadier generals, began selecting company officers, who then encouraged the men to re-enlist, but without success – by 30 December only 9649 men had done so, followed by another 2800 by the end of January. The men also rejected attempts to create 'national' regiments, and Washington was forced to urge the New England assemblies to organise drafts and allow free negroes to re-enlist. Throughout the last four months of the siege, militia, particularly from nearby Massachusetts towns, had to fill the gaps (though they only agreed to do so for short peri-

'Yankee Doodles in their Intrenchments' – a satirical view of the besiegers. Like their regular opponents, mythology has overcome fact in depicting them as wily, sharp-shooting, frontiersmen. Indeed, when such types arrived at Boston in the form of the independent rifle companies, their backwoods ways and habits soon nauseated their pious, civilised, New England cousins. (Anne S K Brown Military Collection, Brown University Library)

ods). By March, the 27 Continental regiments had 14,400 officers and men (including 3000 sick, 10 per cent of which were in hospital, whilst a further 1300 were on detachment).

As acute as the lack of men was the paucity of supplies, despite the capture of British stores. This was especially true of muskets – on 9 December 1775 the Connecticut men were paraded to confiscate the weapons of those not re-enlisting. Combined with the slowness in attaining basic efficiency due to constant reorganisation, it was probably as well that Washington did not have to face Howe in open battle.

ARTILLERY

The nature of North America, and the lack of specialists, greatly influenced the development of the other arms. Before 1775, militia artillery units (like Boston's Ancient and Honourable Artillery Company) were based in fortified towns and trained by their regular colleagues. The Massachusetts Provincial Congress tried to form six new companies by giving cannon to militia regiments, but in May it authorised a ten-company regiment under the experienced Richard Gridley. Each company had five officers (mainly from Boston artillery units), three sergeants, three corporals, six bombardiers, six gunners and 32 matrosses, with a logistical staff and a company of artificers (skilled workmen). The regiment was joined by a Rhode Island company (under another Bostonian), with five officers, a conductor, two sergeants, two bombardiers, four gunners, four corporals, four drummers and fifers and 75 privates, armed with four field guns and 12 heavy guns. New Hampshire and Connecticut both supplied guns, but no gunners to man them.

Three Massachusetts companies armed with 4-pdrs fought at Bunker's Hill, but performed poorly, and in November Congress merged the artillery into a single 12-company regiment, companies theoretically having five officers and 58 men, but bombardiers, gunners and matrosses were kept in proportion to actual strength. Knox replaced Gridley, and he and Washington were given *carte blanche* over organisation; by 1776, the artillery had improved enough to help end the siege.

CAVALRY

North America was considered unsuitable for conventional 'heavy' cavalry, but some colonies created mounted units, or added 'light troops' — effectively mounted infantry — to some militia regiments (the cost of a riding, as opposed to a working, horse, meant such units generally consisted of wealthier citizens). Troops from two regiments, as well as individuals on horseback, attacked the British on 19 April 1775, but little further use was made of them. Congress considered raising mounted units during the siege, but limited resources and the static nature of operations caused the idea to be shelved.

LEXINGTON AND CONCORD 19 APRIL 1775

The 64th Foot had arrived in Boston in 1768. This Private is from one of the Battalion Companies of this unit. (Gerry Embleton)

THE MARCH TO LEXINGTON COMMON

During the afternoon of 18 April, mounted British officers left to patrol the roads between Cambridge and Concord. Seeing one group, led by Major Mitchell (5th), pass through Menotomy, a Lexington 'minuteman', Sergeant William Munroe, organised a guard for the house in which Adams and Hancock were staying; but the patrol rode through Lexington and past Hartwell's Tavern, before turning back, around 2030. By now, the only people ignorant of events were the regulars themselves.

At about 2200, the 700 men of Gage's 21 flank companies were woken and led to the Common, where the boats were waiting. The lack of proper planning was soon obvious: companies were late, their commander, Lieutenant Colonel Francis Smith (10th) was among the last to arrive, and only the intervention of the 23rd's adjutant prevented total chaos. After crossing the Back Bay to Lechemere Point, the men waded ashore (the boats were too heavily laden to be beached) and waited three hours while ammunition and food was distributed, before finally setting off at 0200.

Revere, having arranged the signal in the Old North church, rode towards Cambridge, but a patrol forced him to detour and he reached Lexington at midnight. There, he was joined by William Dawes, who had ridden across Boston Neck and through Roxbury and Cambridge – together with Dr Samuel Prescott, a Concord physician, they set off to rouse the countryside. Revere was captured by Mitchell's patrol (which had already intercepted three other riders) three miles beyond Lexington, but Dawes and Prescott both escaped and continued their mission. Alarmed by Revere's claim that every militia company for 50 miles was alerted, Mitchell returned to Lexington, where he released Revere (who went to help Adams and Hancock escape), and headed off to meet Smith, who, by 0300, had just passed through Menotomy.

The senior militia officer at Lexington, Captain John Parker, had sent four scouts to locate the regulars; three were captured, but the fourth returned, reporting that Smith was only half a mile away. Parker formed his men – most of whom had been in Buckman's Tavern since 0100, having first assembled when Revere arrived – in a two-deep line across the

Encampment on Boston Common. The painting shows the Common in 1768, when British troops first arrived in Boston and were still a novelty; John Hancock's house is on the right, just below Beacon Hill. The scene had changed little by 1775, as Boston's Selectmen refused to provide quarters, or materials for the soldiers to build their own (despite the protection they gave local brick manufacturers during violent wage disputes with their labourers). (Phelps Stokes Collection, New York Public Library)

Bedford road (along which Adams and Hancock had earlier fled). As they lined up, they could see the British advance guard, under Major Thomas Pitcairn of the Marines, approaching the common.

Pitcairn's two leading companies (4th and 10th) were expecting trouble after Mitchell's pessimistic report. They swung to the right of the Meeting House and deployed into line, while Pitcairn rode to the left, ordering the militia to lay down their arms and leave. Parker, realising the odds, told his men to disperse, but to keep their arms, and as they did so, a single shot rang out, then a volley from the regulars. A dozen militia tried to return the fire, but the troops (mostly inexperienced and with months – even years – of Bostonian provocation behind them) became uncontrollable. Ignoring their officers, they charged with the bayonet and Smith, arriving with the main body, had to find a drummer to beat the recall. When order was restored, eight of Parker's men lay dead, and ten more were wounded – British casualties were one sergeant and Pitcairn's horse both slightly wounded. The time was a little after 0500.* At about the same time, two companies of Lincoln 'minute men' (whose commander had been roused by Dr Prescott) reached Concord, along with men from Groton and Bedford. When news of Lexington arrived, 150 men marched out to find the regulars and met them a mile from town. Seeing themselves outnumbered, the militia turned about and created a bizarre spectacle by leading the regulars into Concord, with the fifes and drums of both formations playing away. Smith noticed more militia on a ridge (about 60 ft high) to his right and sent out flanking parties. The Americans withdrew to a second ridge, north

---

*Who fired the first shot? Evidence suggests that it was not anyone on the Common; it may have been a tipsy straggler coming from Buckman's Tavern, but the finger of suspicion points most strongly at someone acting on orders from Samuel Adams. Why else would Parker, a veteran of the French and Indian Wars, line his men up in the open in such a tactically pointless and suicidal position, to face a column of regulars they themselves estimated at over 2000? Adams' comment on hearing the news ('Oh, what a glorious morning!') certainly begs the question as to whether Parker's men were sacrificed for political ends.

This view of Concord in 1776 shows shows the town centre looking west from the cemetery, as it was on 19 April. The meeting house is at the extreme left and the Wright Tavern is centre foreground, in front of the mill pond. The road heading into the distance leads to South Bridge. Contrast the widely dispersed buildings here with the compact town in the 19th century engraving of Chappell's painting. (Massachusetts Historical Society, Boston)

A view of Lexington Green, taken from a 1794 issue of the Massachusetts Magazine, (as was the Concord view). It shows (right to left) the belfry, the three-storey meeting house and the Buckman Tavern, with its outbuildings. The only other building on the common was a schoolhouse, which was just out of picture at the right. (Massachusetts Historical Society, Boston)

of the town (opposite North Bridge), from where Colonel James Barrett, commander of the Concord militia, ordered them back across the Concord River to Punkatasset Hill. The light infantry responded by felling Concord's 'liberty pole', then rejoined the grenadiers on the road. Smith

THE ROAD TO CONCORD

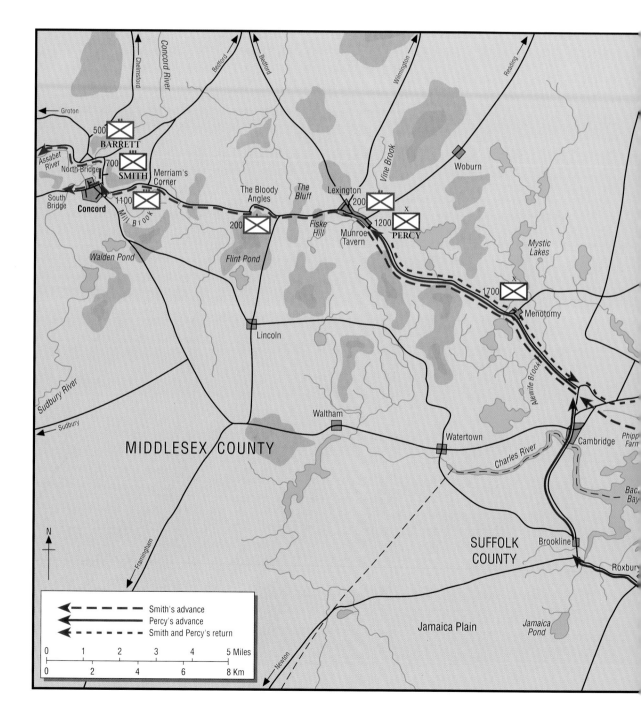

and Pitcairn entered the cemetery and observed the surrounding country-side, noting 'vast numbers assembling in many parts'. Smith ordered the grenadiers to search the town and sent three companies under Captain Pole (10th) to the South Bridge and seven light companies under Captain Parsons (10th) to the North Bridge.

THE ACTION AT NORTH BRIDGE

Parsons left three of the seven companies at the bridge under Captain Laurie (43rd), and took the other four to search Barrett's farm, two miles to the west, where stores had been hidden in the house and the sur-rounding woods and fields. Meanwhile, Laurie sent two companies (4th and 10th) over to the far bank, keeping his on the other side, near Elisha Jones' house (which contained 55 barrels of beef and 1700 pounds of salt fish).

In Concord, the search yielded little, largely due to the excessive care taken not to offend civilians or damage property, and a certain amount of gullibility on the regulars' behalf. Some 500 pounds of musket balls were dumped in the Mill Pond behind Wright's Tavern (wherein Smith and Pitcairn had their headquarters), but most were later recovered. At South Bridge, Pole had better luck, damaging three iron 24-pdrs, destroying flour and setting fire to gun carriages and wooden tools. This fire, and those started in two other houses (but extinguished after complaints by their owners) would have unexpected consequences.

The Battle of Lexington. One of the four famous prints by militiaman Amos Doolittle, from drawings and interviews of eyewitnesses. The 4th and 10th Foot fire on Parker's dispersing men, with Pitcairn at right on horseback. None of the militia are firing back, and it was clearly the artist's intention to make out that the British fired without provoca-tion. In contrast, later works fed on the 'embattled farmers' image, with more and more men returning the British fire. (Anne S K Brown Military Collection, Brown University Library)

A View of the Town of Concord. Smith and Pitcairn observe the local militia falling back across the ridges, east of Concord, to their muster ground on Punkatasset Hill. Although much cruder, and drawn from slightly altered perspectives, the similarities between this illustration and the drawing from 1794 are obvious. (Anne S K Brown Military Collection, Brown University Library)

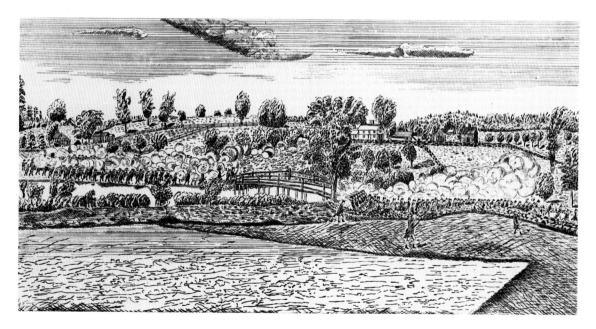

The Engagement at the North Bridge in Concord. As the militia attack from the west, the regulars attempt a manoeuvre known as 'street firing', by which a column could defend a narrow passage. The leading ranks would fire, then file to the rear to reform and reload. Sadly, the lack of a common drill book led to utter confusion and forced the three British companies to retreat (not forgetting that they were outnumbered five to one). (Anne S K Brown Military Collection, Brown University Library)

COMMANDING

Lieutenant Colonel Francis Smith, 10th Foot

GRENADIERS
Lieutenant Colonel Smith (about 385 rank-and-file)[1] 10th[2], 4th, 18th, 38th, 47th, 52nd, 59th, Marines[3], 43rd, 23rd, 5th Foot

LIGHT COMPANIES
Major Pitcairn, Marines (about 350 rank-and-file) 10th, 4th, 23rd, 43rd, Marines, 59th, 52nd, 47th, 38th, 5th Foot

RELIEF FORCE
(*Brigadier General Lord Percy*, 5th Foot)
I Brigade (Battalion companies only):
4th Foot – Lt Col Madison (315)[4]
47th Foot – Lt Col Nesbit (296)
Marines – Maj Pitcairn (336)

23rd Foot – Lt Col Bernard (314)

RESERVE[5]
Battalion companies 10th, 64th Foot

Notes:
1. Rough estimate based on 35 corporals and privates per company (theoretically 39, but undoubtedly lower due to shortages of manpower in their parent units).
2. Orders of march based on eyewitness accounts and the usual 'form' for assembling troops according to seniority – oldest regiment at the front, or far right, second oldest at the rear, or far left, then alternating front/right and rear/left, towards the centre. As Smith was CO of the 10th, the flank companies of his regiment probably took the 'post of honour' (if not, they would have been immediately next to the 4th).
3. The Marines ranked between the 49th and 50th Foot; there is some doubt whether their flank companies went with Smith, or with Percy's brigade; this would make Pitcairn's presence hard to explain, but if so, the flank companies of the 52nd and 59th would swap.
4. Rank-and-file strengths for 30 March 1775.
5. Sent over to Charlestown peninsula in the evening.

At 0900, Barrett, now with almost 500 men, saw the smoke and, fearing the worst, marched towards Concord, giving his men strict orders not to fire first. Laurie's two detached companies withdrew over North Bridge, and he sent for reinforcements, but the militia's rapid advance denied him time to form, or for his men to remove the planks of the bridge. Attempting a complicated manoeuvre unfamiliar to his colleagues, his leading company masked the fire of the others and a half-hearted volley caused only two fatalities. The militia's reply killed two regulars and wounded ten (including four of the eight officers) and, led by Major John Buttrick, they forced Laurie back over 400 yards onto the three companies of grenadiers Smith had eventually collected. Now the militia withdrew, and Smith uncertain what to do next, returned to Concord.

Pole heard the firing and also returned, his men pulling up the bridge after them; in Concord, the grenadiers commandeered horses, carriages and bedding to carry the wounded. Parsons, meanwhile, had recrossed North Bridge unmolested, having found no stores and heard no gunfire, and only became aware of events on finding a dead regular (apparently scalped by a youth, whom he had surprised).

At noon, Smith withdrew, despatching flanking parties to the ridge north of the road, to cover the main force. Barrett's men saw this and set off across the fields north of Concord towards Merriam's Corner (where the Lexington and Old Bedford roads meet) to join companies from Reading and other nearby towns, until there were over 1100 Americans in the fields around the Merriam house. As the British flankers briefly rejoined the column to cross a small bridge, someone fired; the regulars fired an ineffectual volley, but the militia's response left two dead and several wounded near the stream, and gave Smith an idea of what the next 16 miles had in store.

Phase 5 (1000)
Smith eventually leads reinforcements to rescue Lawrie.
These drive back the Militia
who retire to Punktasset Hill

Phase 1 (0600)
Militia observe British marching
towards Concord. They withdraw to a
ridge north of the town opposite
North Bridge

Phase 3 (0700)
Pole's command search area
around South Bridge. They set
fire to gun carriages and
wooden tools

COL. BARRETT'S FARM

ASSABET RIVER

6

LEE'S HILL
4

OLD MANSE

SOUTH BRIDGE
3
5
SUDBURY RIVER
2

8

SUDBURY

CONCORD CEMETERY
WRIGHT'S TAVERN
1
MEETING HOUSE

Phase 4 (0900)
Pole hears firing at North
Bridge and withdraws into
Concord after pulling up
planks of South Bridge

MILL POND

WALTHAM

Phase 2 (0600)
The British enter Concord and the
Grenadiers begin searching the
town. Smith despatches Parsons
and seven companies to North
Bridge and Pole and three companies to South Bridge

Phase 7 (1230)
British withdraw from Concord. Light
infantry along the ridge, Grenadiers
and wounded along the road

X

SMITH

BRITISH TROOPS

1 Lt.Col. Smith & Maj. Pitcairn with the
Grenadiers and Marines
2-5 Capt. Pole with the Light Coys. of the 47th
and 59th Foot and the Grenadier Coy. of the
10th Foot
3 Light Coy. 59th
4 Light Coy. 47th
5 Gren. Coy. 10th
6 Capt. Parsons with the Light Coys. of the 5th,
38th, 52nd and 23rd Foot
7 Capt. Laurie with the Light Coys. of the 4th
10th and 43rd Foot
8 Lt.Col. Smith leading the Grenadiers of the
23rd, 47th and 5th Foot to reinforce Laurie

BRITISH FACINGS

4th 5th 10th 18/65th 23rd 38th 43rd 47th Mar 52nd 39th

Coat
Facings

Phase 6 (1200)
Parson's command return from searching Barrett's Farm

Phase 2 (0600)
Barrett orders the militia to withdraw across the Concord River and to assemble on Punkatasset Hill

Phase 4 (0900)
Barrett now has nearly 500 men. Seeing smoke from the fires he marches towards Concord. Buttrick leads attack on Lawrie's command, driving it back towards Concord

X
BARRETT

Phase 7 (1230)
As they see the British retire the Militia on Punkatasset Hill re-cross the river and head over the Great Fields to Merriam's Corner

PUNKATASSET HILL

CONCORD RIVER

NORTH BRIDGE

7

ELISHA JONES' HOUSE

BEDFORD

THE GREAT FIELDS

OLD BEDFORD ROAD

Phase 6 (1200)
At about this time American reinforcements begin to arrive down the Old Bedford Road

MERRIAM HOUSE

MILL BROOK

MERRIAM'S CORNER

Phase 6 (1200)
Other militia start to gather at Merriam's Corner to await the British withdrawal

LEXINGTON

N

CONCORD AND ENVIRONS

19 April 1775, 0600-1230, viewed from the south-east showing the British arrival at Concord, the action at North Bridge and the subsequent withdrawal towards Merriam's Corner. (The dark green areas show swamp/marshes)

CONCORD[1]

Acton (3 companies)	mm	100 (at least)[2]
Bedford (2 companies)	mm	79
Concord (4 companies)	mm	200 (at least)
Lincoln (1 company)	mm	62
Other individuals	—	50 (at least)

MERRIAM'S CORNER[3]

Billerica (3 companies)	—	101	
Chelmsford (2 companies)	—	104	
Framingham (3 companies)	mm	149	
Reading (4 companies)	mm	291	
Sudbury (6 companies)	mm	237	
Woburn (3 companies)	—	254	
Dracot (2 companies)	—	127	
Stow (1 company)	—	81	Arrived too late to take part
Westford (3 companies)	—	113	

AT LINCOLN

Lexington (1 company)	mm	120[4]
Cambridge (1 company)	—	77

AT LEXINGTON

Newton (3 companies)	—	219

AT MENOTOMY (ARLINGTON)

Arlington (1 company)	—	52
Beverley (3 companies)	mm	122
Brookline (3 companies)	—	150 (at least)
Danvers (8 companies)	mm	281
Dedham (8 companies)	—	337
Lynn (5 companies)	mm	248
Malden (1 company)	—	76
Medford(1 company)	—	59
Needham (3 companies)	—	185
Roxbury (3 companies)	—	140
Watertown (1 company)	—	134

Notes:
1. Places at which substantial numbers of militia entered the action; individuals and small groups were constantly arriving during the day.
2. The details given are geographical origin of unit, number of companies, number of effectives engaged and if the unit was one of minute men (mm) – where there were several companies, the designation of the majority has been used.
3. All Concord troops were also at Merriam's Corner.
4. John Parker's company, reformed.

THE WITHDRAWAL TO BOSTON

With no command structure present above company level (and none existing above regimental level), the militia could not destroy Smith's force, but it could certainly inflict many casualties from positions of relative safety, and possibly even dictate Smith's route. The British had to keep to the roads and their flank guards would only be effective as long as the terrain allowed them to keep the column out of enemy musket range, and their

A View of the south part of Lexington. Having rescued Smith's column, Percy's brigade withdraws under harassing fire from groups of militia (note the British flanking parties and their formation). Burning houses are clearly visible – another important propaganda element – apparently it was a far more heinous crime to destroy personal property than to use it as cover from which to kill the King's soldiers. (Anne S K Brown Military Collection, Brown University Library)

own ammunition held out. Unless help arrived, things looked grim for the regulars.

At a hill a mile from Meriam's Corner, the column was ambushed by a Sudbury company in cover at the roadside. As the regulars crossed Tanner's Brook and turned sharp left between two copses, more 'minute men' (including a Bedford company) killed eight of them, but this time the British hit back. The Bedford company lost its captain and two others to light infantrymen coming round behind them (a tactic that would account for almost two-thirds of all militia fatalities by the day's end). More men were lost half a mile further on, as the column passed Hartwell's Tavern, and the homes of Samuel Hartwell and Captain William Smith. The severity of the fighting from the hill to these three houses led to this section of road being called the 'Bloody Angles'.

After exchanging fire once again with Parker's Lexington 'minute men' (though with far less effect than earlier), the British ransacked the Bull Tavern and headed on to a 20-foot high bluff, and then to Fiske Hill (80 feet high). As Smith's men climbed the west side of Fiske Hill, he decided to rally them and placed a rearguard on the Bluff while the main body halted in the road to reform. But a lack of ammunition, and the heavy fire, proved too much; as Smith fell, wounded in the leg, order disintegrated. The column 'began to run rather than retreat in order', climbing the 120 feet to the summit of Concord Hill, before covering the remaining mile to Lexington Common, where three wounded were abandoned.

Smith's command stumbled through Lexington, fatigued and racked with thirst, finally having been reformed by the officers blocking the road in front and presenting their bayonets at the men. Half a mile east of the common, they found a relief column, commanded by Lord Percy; Smith's men collapsed on the ground while the wounded were taken to the Munroe Tavern.

Percy had spent the previous night on Boston Common, listening to the townspeople discussing Smith's mission. He reported this to Gage, who agreed to provide Smith with support, and at 0400, Percy was ordered to assemble his brigade. Unfortunately, the aide delivering orders to the Marines left them at Pitcairn's quarters, unaware of his absence. It was 0900 before the Marines finally assembled and Percy's brigade could leave.

Near Cambridge, Percy had again found the bridge over the Charles River taken up, but the planks had been stored on the far side and he soon had a narrow section relaid (having experienced exactly this on 30 March, he had come prepared with wagons full of tools and spare planks, but they were not needed and returned to Boston). His men filed across, leaving two supply wagons to follow, and reaching Lexington around noon, he sited his two cannon on the low hills east of the village and set up his head-quarters in William Munroe's tavern.

Now, at 1500, Percy could see groups of militia behind walls and build-ings. He ordered the guns to open fire, deployed marksmen in front of his line and had six nearby buildings fired to prevent the Americans using them as cover (later cited as one of the day's greatest atrocities). At about the same time, Major General William Heath and Dr Warren, arrived in Lexington. Neither had much grasp of tactics, and the militia were too dis-persed for them to exercise any control (even if there had been a suitable chain of command), so they limited themselves to offering encouragement to those in their immediate vicinity. Around 1530, the British left Lexington, with Smith's men leading and Percy's four battalions taking turns to cover the flanks and rear. As they entered Menotomy, where the local alarm company had ambushed Percy's two supply wagons, more mili-tia arrived, swelling their number to 2000 from 35 companies.

This part of the withdrawal saw some of the bloodiest fighting with hand-to-hand combat in buildings and fields. Jason Russell's house boast-ed the most men to die in one place all day – 11 'minute men' (all killed in one room), two regulars and Russell himself. A mile beyond the Menotomy River, more 'minute men' waited behind a pile of barrels; a flanking party took them by surprise, killing three, including Major Isaac Gardner from Brookline, the most senior fatality on either side. Some 20 militia, and as many regulars, were killed between the Russell house and Cooper's Tavern, and over 40 British and 25 Americans died in Menotomy.

As the withdrawal continued Percy realised that only an hour's day-light remained and his column was still some way from Boston. He knew the road through Cambridge would take too long and might be blocked, so he decided to head for Charlestown, where the warships' guns could pro-tect him and their boats could ferry his exhausted men back to their barracks. It was an inspired (or fortunate) choice – the bridge over the Charles River had indeed been dismantled again, and now there were plen-ty of militia to defend it, but those on the road to Charlestown were too

This Corporal is from the Grenadier Company of the 47th Foot, a unit which had been in the colonies since 1773. (Gerry Embleton)

Withdrawal from Concord. This engraving, after the painting by Alonzo Chappell, illustrates the close-quarter nature of the fighting along the road back to Boston. It is unlikely, though, that the militia used the tactics shown, preferring to shoot from cover and work in small groups, rather than the company-sized unit seen in the field to the left. The artist has not missed the opportunity to show the inevitable burning buildings. (Anne S K Brown Military Collection, Brown University Library)

few and inexperienced to attack him frontally, though he was forced to unlimber his cannon several times.

As the sun set just after 1900, the regulars came to a small pond, where many threw themselves in to quench their thirst and refresh their sweating bodies. Once past Prospect Hill and over Charlestown Neck, Percy's brigade occupied Bunker's Hill, while Smith's exhausted men went into the town. Though the town's militia had not marched out, the settlement's Selectmen were worried at the mood of the troops and negotiated a truce with Percy, who would hold the regulars in check, while the townspeople helped Smith's men onto the ferry.

Gage sent over two regiments (10th and 64th) to perform guard duty on the peninsula, while plans were made for defences to be built immediately across the Neck and on Bunker's Hill. The day had begun with frustrating delays and ended in frantic activity, driven almost by blind panic at the thought of 20,000 to 30,000 well-armed (if leaderless and unco-ordinated) militia waiting to sweep the British back into the harbour.

American losses were 49 dead, 41 wounded and 5 missing; the British had had 73 killed, 174 wounded and 26 missing (mainly captured), and most units would need several days to recover. However, the greatest casualty was the idea that the militia could not oppose them – albeit, the former had fought on their own ground (even in their own homes), and the terrain had ideally suited the only type of warfare at which they were superior. Despite the courage and fortitude shown in marching over 50 miles without food or rest, the regulars (principally the flank companies) had been ill-disciplined on occasions and had fired too high, causing few casualties – a sign of inexperienced troops. Some looting had occurred, despite – occasionally because of – the efforts of junior officers, though most 'looting legends' were either political propaganda, or the contemporary equivalent of insurance frauds!

BOSTON BESIEGED

Over the next two days, over 20,000 men gathered around Boston; despite having no semblance of order, they were enough in number to panic Gage into deciding that he was too weak to hold anything more than the town itself and, ignoring the advice of Graves and others (who also recommended fortifying Dorchester Heights to deny it to the enemy), he withdrew from Charlestown peninsula. Montresor's works were left unfinished and Gage negotiated with the Provincial Congress for Bostonians to leave (without arms) if local Loyalists were allowed through the American lines. He soon realised that the agreement left the Americans free to bombard Boston, and eventually put an end to it (those Americans remaining in Boston would also give the Committee of Safety useful intelligence).

The Massachusetts Provincial Congress now attempted to form an 'army of observation' from its own troops and those of the other three New England contingents which had responded to its call for help. Major General Artemas Ward was given command, and he made his headquarters at Cambridge, around which he based two-thirds of the Massachusetts and Connecticut regiments, and the New Hampshire contingent (who were protecting his left flank around Medford).

Major General John Thomas was sent to command the southern wing around Roxbury, which included the remaining Massachusetts and Connecticut units and all the Rhode Island force, when it arrived. Despite commanding the more exposed of the two wings, Thomas refused to construct defensive works, or occupy Dorchester Neck when Ward recommended it.

April and May were full of false alarms, emphasising the lack of leadership on both sides; the Committee of Safety put the province's militia on full alert and ordered drafts from local units to reinforce Ward. Major General Israel Putnam had an answer to the boredom which inspired many of these alerts – he had his Connecticut men build three forts, two protecting the much-dismantled (and only) bridge over the Charles River, and the other blocking the roads into Cambridge from Charlestown Neck and Lechmere Point. On 13 May, he marched almost 3000 men onto Breed's Hill, where they drilled before marching into Charlestown to taunt the crew of HMS *Somerset*, anchored in the ferryway between Charlestown and Boston with its guns loaded, waiting for the Americans to fire. Nothing happened, but shortly afterwards, the remaining inhabitants of Charlestown slipped away without anyone noticing.

Meanwhile, the Second Continental Congress had convened in Philadelphia to discuss a common response to the events of 19 April. The New England delegates managed to convince the gathering that it was vital for Congress to adopt the army around Boston, both to counter the accusation that this was a purely regional struggle and to broaden the base of the war effort. Eventually, Congress agreed, adopting the 'army of observation' and making the first moves towards appointing a commander-in-chief.

On 17 May, a fire – possibly started deliberately – destroyed one of the wharf areas holding the weapons and clothing of some companies of the 47th and 65th. Meanwhile, Ward's officers, having reconnoitred the hills around Boston, recommended the construction of works to defend the approaches to Cambridge and a strong redoubt, with cannon, on Bunker's Hill. Neither the Committee of Safety, nor Ward himself, felt capable of making a decision on either suggestion, and nothing more was done, but Dr Church kept Gage fully informed and his subsequent inaction may have been encouraged by this indecision.

On 18 May, Gage's recently-arrived Adjutant General, Lieutenant Colonel James Abercrombie, went up the Charles River in a ship's boat, only to be driven back by musket fire from the banks. It was the first reconnaissance by the British since 19 April, and the last until July.

In January, Gage had put the garrison on salt rations for four days each week, and though supplies still arrived from England, fresh food was short. Yet for some reason – possibly his feelings for private property – over 1000 head of livestock were left grazing on islands in the harbour. Finally, on 20 May, he sent 30 men in an unarmed schooner to secure hay from Grape Island (nine miles south-east of Boston). An attempt by Thomas to intercept them with 300 men in boats failed, but they took care to burn the rest of the hay on the island.

Four days later, the Committee of Safety decided to remove all livestock from Noddle's and Hog's Islands, north of Boston. Gage was informed and told Graves, who kept his naval stores in a rented building on Noddle's Island. Graves increased the guard-boat patrols but recommended an Army garrison be put ashore; Gage refused to consider it. On 28 May, an American detachment began setting fire to barns and pastures on the island and killing any livestock they could not remove. Graves sent HMS *Diana* (under the command of his nephew, Lieutenant Thomas Graves) to cut off their retreat and land Marines on the island. Gage, believing it was a trap, failed to support the naval move, and the Americans duly escaped to Hog Island, supported by Putnam who had brought more men and two small cannon across the Mystic River.

Fighting continued until sunset, when the British withdrew; unfortunately, the *Diana* had been stranded on a sandbank and, despite attempts to row her off, she was burnt to the waterline (but not until the Americans had removed four of her guns). The total casualties amounted to one or two dead and a few wounded on each side. Graves eventually rescued his stores, but the Americans nevertheless finished destroying the buildings on the two islands and also cleared the remaining livestock from Deer Island, and Peddock's Island at the southern end of the harbour.

As the two armies sparred with each other, the regulars became more frustrated and the Americans more cocksure (some officers wildly estimated 300 British dead from the fight on Noddle's Island alone). In weapons, training and morale, they were about equal; where the British should have had an undoubted advantage was in staff work and leadership of large formations, but their operations to date had been riddled with negligence and incompetence. Orders were mislaid or unsupervised, returns needed to calculate the garrison's food and supplies never reached London, and no attempt was made to use those civilians loyal to the King to gather intelligence. Two incidents summed up the avoidable chaos – when the converged flank battalions were ordered into a separate camp on 5 June, there were neither plans, nor officers, to show them where to go; and in May or June, all Gage's papers and correspondence were stolen from the Governor's House in the town.

On 8 June, Gage finally acceded to Graves' requests and ordered 200 light infantry to Noddle's Island to secure the remaining hay and supplies, but the Rebels had burned the island and little of value was retrieved.

BREED'S HILL: 17 JUNE

The 17th Light Dragoons, to which this Private in dis-mounted order belongs, landed in Boston from Ireland shortly before Breed's Hill. (Gerry Embleton)

CHARLESTOWN PENINSULA OCCUPIED

At the end of May, a convoy bringing reinforcements across the Atlantic began to straggle into harbour, including, on 25 May, the frigate HMS *Cerberus* carrying both orders for Gage to place Massachusetts under martial law, and three major generals – Howe, Clinton and Burgoyne. Chosen as experienced fighting officers, they were promoted only in 1772 and had never served at that grade; until Gage gave them commands, all they could do was study the situation and develop their own ideas.

On 12 June, Gage declared martial law, offering pardons to all except John Hancock and Samuel Adams; meanwhile, he and his generals planned a four-pronged attack on Dorchester Heights, Roxbury, Charlestown and Cambridge, scheduled for Sunday 18 June. Inevitably, word reached the Committee of Safety and, on 15 June, it met and resolved to occupy Bunker's Hill and the hills behind Dorchester (ironically, none of this reached Gage, as Dr Church was in Philadelphia with despatches too secret to be entrusted to anyone else).

Ward convened a council of war the next day, attended mostly by junior officers, confident and aggressive after recent events. Despite misgivings, Ward bowed to the majority and ordered detachments from four regiments (three Massachusetts, and one Connecticut), plus two guns, to occupy Charlestown peninsula.*

Around 2100 on 16 June, the Massachusetts contingent left Cambridge Common, led by Colonels William Prescott and Richard Gridley. Collecting Captain Thomas Knowlton's detachment and several wagons carrying entrenching tools, they crossed Charlestown Neck, but on reaching Bunker's Hill, a long argument (involving Putnam) led to a decision to place the main work on Breed's Hill, with supporting works only on Bunker's Hill. Gridley marked out an area about 130 ft square, with a redan (triangular projection) facing Charlestown, and a narrow gorge on the

*The absence of any written record of these orders has aroused controversy over whether the occupation of Breed's Hill was intentional, a mistake (by Prescott) or deliberate disobedience by Prescott and others (possibly encouraged by Putnam).

opposite side, to allow easy access. Work began at midnight, and despite the exposed position and guard boats in the harbour, there were no alarms – such was the state of the garrison that British sentries heard the digging, but reported nothing, only mentioning it in passing conversation the next day!

At 0400, the *Lively* spotted the earthworks on Breed's Hill and opened fire, while the *Glasgow* swung round to cover Charlestown Neck. By 0900 the Copp's Hill battery had joined in the bombardment. Gage and his senior officers agreed that the works posed a threat, but were sufficiently incomplete and isolated to offer a chance to attack. The quickest approach would be by water, but even using every available boat, only half the 2200 men they felt would be needed could be carried at once. As the boats were not purpose-built, flat-bottom, transports, but plain rowing boats with crews of varying quality, and with no special facilities for artillery or horses, it was vital to select a landing site that allowed them in close to land guns and return quickly for the second wave. Moulton's Point offered an open, gently-sloping, beach, a road (of sorts), and was a safe distance from Breed's Hill.

The plan was to bypass the redoubt to the north and capture Bunker's Hill and the Neck. Howe would command, while Clinton supervised the reinforcements, in Boston. The first wave would comprise six battalions, six detached flank companies and the artillery, and would depart from the Long Wharf and the North Battery; two further battalions would be in reserve at the North Battery and the rest of the garrison was to keep itself in readiness. As the operation might take some time, blankets and three days' rations would be issued.

THE BRITISH RESPOND

Howe and Graves then boarded the *Somerset*, but the water was too shallow and Graves had to transfer men from the three larger warships into the sloops and Lieutenant Colonel James's two gondolas. The *Falcon* joined the

Charlestown burning – a watercolour from a drawing made during the battle by an English officer, showing the second wave landing to the north of Charlestown, while the Glasgow (left) and Symmetry fire at troop crossing the Neck. The Army's two gondolas can be seen closer in by the mill dam (note the figures crossing the Boston mill dam, in the foreground). (Emmet Collection, New York Public Library)

Lively (still slowly warping round to Moulton's Point), while the *Symmetry* and the gondolas went to help the *Glasgow* prevent reinforcements crossing the Neck. The Copp's Hill battery kept up a steady fire, hitting the redoubt several times, but doing little damage, due to the range and the thickness of the works.

On Breed's Hill, thirst, hunger (few men had brought rations) and lack of sleep were creating problems. When the *Lively*'s first salvo killed one man, the others stopped work to bury him and a few took the chance to disappear. Others compared the activity in Boston with the empty slope of Bunker's Hill behind, and wondered if they had been betrayed.

Putnam rode over from Cambridge when the firing began and returned to report to Ward. Aware that Gage could strike anywhere, Ward could not commit his forces, but realised Prescott was isolated and ordered up detached companies from three Massachusetts regiments to occupy Charlestown.

At 1300, Prescott's men – and the huge audience on Boston's rooftops and the hills around the harbour – saw a double column of boats slowly appear and row towards the peninsula. As the *Lively*, *Falcon* and *Spitfire* raked Moulton's Point, the *Symmetry* and the two gondolas swept the Neck, the *Glasgow* fired on Charlestown and the 24-pdrs on Copp's Hill engaged the redoubt, the ships having neither the range nor elevation to hit it – a few salvoes from the two small guns in the redoubt were the only reply from the Americans.

Ward, pressed by the Committee of Safety, sent two New Hampshire and nine Massachusetts regiments, with two more companies of artillery, to help Prescott, while more regiments formed a defensive line east of Cambridge. Colonel John Stark, leading the New Hampshire contingent, found his men short of ammunition and had to issue ball and loose powder, then wait while it was made into cartridges before starting the hour's march to the Neck. Prescott, aware of a 200-yard gap between the breastwork and the Mystick River, sent Knowlton, with two guns, to delay the landing, but the gunners 'withdrew' to Bunker's Hill (they returned when Putnam threatened to kill the commanding officer, but later deserted again, abandoning their guns). Knowlton, aware his force was now too small to act offensively, occupied a rail fence, strengthening it with materials from another fence and mown hay from nearby fields. Prescott subsequently despatched two more flanking parties (of whom nothing more was heard), and then lost more men, who took advantage of an order to save the entrenching tools (supposedly given by Putnam) to desert.

By 1500, five Massachusetts regiments had reached the peninsula, but had halted. Stark found them blocking the road and, braving the bombardment of the Neck (in all probability just a few guns firing every few minutes at long range), he led his and Reed's regiments across without loss.

About this time, Howe landed with the second wave and despatched four light companies to cover his deployment, while forming his force into three lines on Moulton's Hill. The enemy position seemed stronger than it had from Boston, running 600 yards from Charlestown to the Mystic River, and with reserves on Bunker's Hill. Immediately ordering reinforcements, he had his artillery bombard the redoubt and ordered the gondolas round

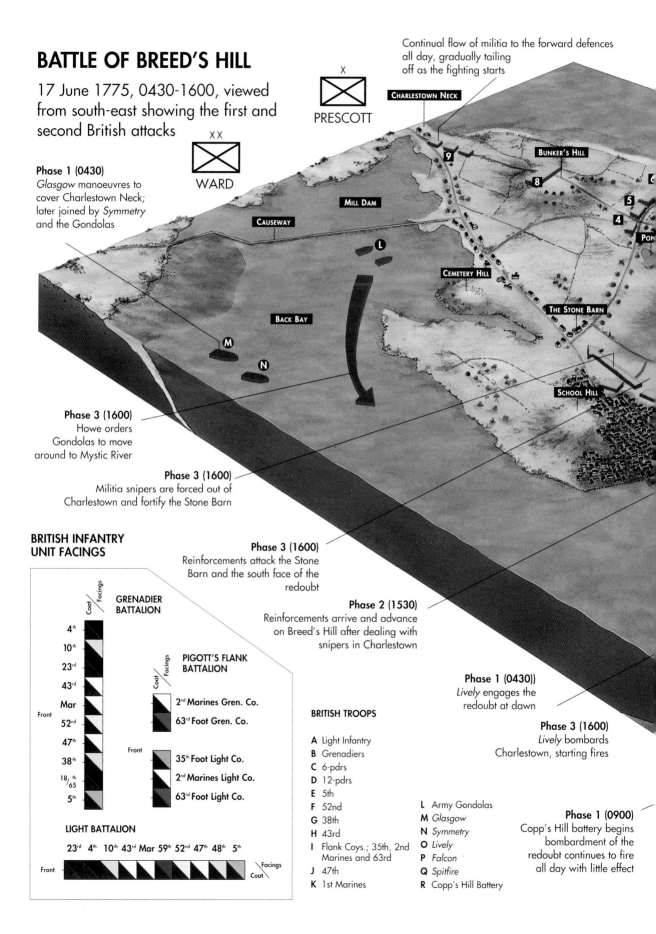

BATTLE OF BREED'S HILL

17 June 1775, 0430-1600, viewed from south-east showing the first and second British attacks

X
PRESCOTT

XX
WARD

Continual flow of militia to the forward defences all day, gradually tailing off as the fighting starts

CHARLESTOWN NECK

BUNKER'S HILL

9

8

5

4

MILL DAM

CAUSEWAY

CEMETERY HILL

PON

L

THE STONE BARN

BACK BAY

M

N

SCHOOL HILL

Phase 1 (0430)
Glasgow manoeuvres to cover Charlestown Neck; later joined by *Symmetry* and the Gondolas

Phase 3 (1600)
Howe orders Gondolas to move around to Mystic River

Phase 3 (1600)
Militia snipers are forced out of Charlestown and fortify the Stone Barn

Phase 3 (1600)
Reinforcements attack the Stone Barn and the south face of the redoubt

Phase 2 (1530)
Reinforcements arrive and advance on Breed's Hill after dealing with snipers in Charlestown

Phase 1 (0430))
Lively engages the redoubt at dawn

Phase 3 (1600)
Lively bombards Charlestown, starting fires

Phase 1 (0900)
Copp's Hill battery begins bombardment of the redoubt continues to fire all day with little effect

BRITISH INFANTRY UNIT FACINGS

GRENADIER BATTALION

Coat / Facings

| 4th |
| 10th |
| 23rd |
| 43rd |
| Mar |
| 52nd |
| 47th |
| 38th |
| 18th/65 |
| 5th |

Front

PIGOTT'S FLANK BATTALION

Coat / Facings

2nd Marines Gren. Co.
63rd Foot Gren. Co.

Front

35th Foot Light Co.
2nd Marines Light Co.
63rd Foot Light Co.

BRITISH TROOPS

A Light Infantry
B Grenadiers
C 6-pdrs
D 12-pdrs
E 5th
F 52nd
G 38th
H 43rd
I Flank Coys.; 35th, 2nd Marines and 63rd
J 47th
K 1st Marines

L Army Gondolas
M *Glasgow*
N *Symmetry*
O *Lively*
P *Falcon*
Q *Spitfire*
R Copp's Hill Battery

LIGHT BATTALION

23rd 4th 10th 43rd Mar 59th 52nd 47th 48th 5th

Front

Facings / Coat

Phase 2 (1530)
The Light infantry attack Stark's wall and are repulsed with heavy loss

Phase 3 (1600)
The Light infantry make a feint against the rail fence

Phase 2 (1530)
The Grenadiers attack rail fence and are beaten back

Phase 3 (1600)
The Grenadiers attack the area around the fleches and are forced to withdraw

Phase 2 (1500)
Royal Artillery 6-pdrs and 35th's Grenadier company are slowed down by marshy ground and fences; also discover that the 6-pdrs have the wrong ammunition

Phase 2 (1500)
12-pdrs on Moulton's Hill begin to bombard the redoubt breastwork

STONE WALL

RAIL FENCE

Ⓐ

MARSHY GROUND

MOULTON'S POINT

THREE FLECHES

Ⓑ   Ⓒ   Ⓓ

MOULTON'S HILL

Ⓔ   BRICK KILNS

SAND BANKS

3

Ⓕ

2

Ⓖ

1

Ⓗ

Ⓘ

BREED'S HILL

Ⓙ

Ⓚ

SECONDARY LANDINGS

Ⓠ

Ⓟ

Main landings at Moulton's Point

Phase 2 (1430)
Falcon and *Spitfire* sweep Moulton's Point with grapeshot

Phase 2 (1530)
Pigott's command moves around to the base of Breed's Hill, coming under sniper fire from Charlestown

CHARLESTOWN

Ⓞ

BOSTON HARBOUR

Phase 3 (1600)
Pigott's command makes a feint attack against the redoubt and breastwork

HOWE

Ⓡ

N

AMERICAN TROOPS

1-2 Redoubt & Breastwork (Prescott's, Frye's, Bridge's Regts.)

3 Fleches (Original occupants unknown but reinforced by parts of Nixon's, Brewer's and Doolittle's Regts. by 1600)

4 Knowlton's Regt. and Trevett's Co. (2 x 4pdrs)

5 Reed's Regt.

6 Stark's Regt.

7 Charlestown (Prescott's, Little's Doolittle's Woodbridge's – detachments of each; retired to the Stone Barn about 1600 when town set on fire)

8 Bunker's Hill (Putnam with various Massachusetts contingents)

9 Reinforcements (Gerrish's, Gardner's and 3 Connecticut Cos.)

The cyclorama of the Battle of Bunker Hill was produced for the centenary by a group of European artists and exhibited until its mysterious disappearance – these eight plates, run over the next three pages, are all that remain (though another set of three shows a similar, but notice-ably different, work). The whole represents the final assault, around 1630, and is marred only by a tendency to turn every British ship into a three-deck man-of-war and a misrepresentation of the numbers of men on each side.

The grenadiers and 52nd Foot storm the breastwork, which extended about 110 yards north of the redoubt. Both it and the redoubt were rough and incomplete, but were about six feet high with a ditch in front and a fir-ing platform inside. Critics of the British plans have argued that occupying Charlestown Neck would have won a bloodless victory. However, the south side was imprac-ticable, as the mill dam and marshes would have pre-vented the boats from getting close enough to land artillery; the north side was a long row up the Mystic River, (which remained uncharted, due to an oversight by Graves), against the tide, leaving the first wave unsup-ported for almost two hours, while the boats returned to reload.

British artillery fire enfilades the breastwork, forcing the defenders back to the redoubt, while the 5th Foot attack the fleches and the remaining light infantry demonstrate against the rail fence. Howe's battlefield tactics have also been widely criticised, but he correctly identified the weak points of his opponents' line and attacked them.

Only bad luck with the wrong artillery ammunition at a crucial moment, and fate placing Stark, one of the few competent American officers, at the most vulnerable part of the line, prevented either of the first two attacks from clearing the field.

The 38th and 43rd Foot attack the redoubt's eastern face; the gesticulating officer in the long coat by the cannon, is Prescott, while the well-dressed, bareheaded man in the right centre foreground, hat in hand, may possibly be Dr Warren. In the background, the 2nd Marines and 63rd land on the beach. Although Charlestown's wharves and jetties would have offered a perfect beachhead, any landing would have been under the redoubt's guns and would have forced the troops to then fight their way through the town, negating their tactical superiority in manoeuvre and firepower.

As the 47th Foot attack the large barn fortified by some of the Americans driven out of Charlestown, the 1st Marines storm the south face of the redoubt and its redan. Fear, dense smoke from hundreds of black-powder weapons, and the claustrophobic nature of the fighting around the redoubt, led to the myth that the battle was fought in a heat wave. In fact, humidity was low and the temperature was 64 degrees Fahrenheit in the morning, reaching the 80s by mid-afternoon – a typical June day in Boston. Although both sides had around 2000 men engaged, stories that the redoubt was held by only 150 men abounded at the time the cyclorama was painted, and are reflected in the numbers depicted on each side. (The Bostonian Society, Old State House, Boston)

to the Mystick River (which forced them to move against the tide and effectively put them out of action for the rest of the day).

The ground before him seemed perfectly straightforward – fields, clumps of trees, and some brick kilns. In reality, it was rocky and uneven, with hidden gulleys and stout fences; these would remain hidden until the advance, as neither Gage nor Lieutenant Montresor had examined the area previously. Worse still, no horses had been brought over for Howe or his staff, denying him the chance to reconnoitre the ground (which would also have disclosed the yawning gap on Prescott's left).

Soon that gap was filled: Stark's main body joined Knowlton at the rail fence and spilled down the nine foot embankment onto the beach, where they built a wall of stones while Stark set up an aiming point 50 yards in front. The line was now complete, with over 4000 men:

- the Massachusetts detachments (equal to two regiments, but with no overall commander) defending Charlestown and covering the redoubt.
- the redoubt and a breastwork (stretching 110 yards north of the redoubt to cover its left flank) held by Massachusetts troops under Prescott.
- the gap between the redoubt and rail fence covered by three *fleches* (hastily-built from fence material), fences and trees along the road.
- the rail fence manned by New Hampshire and Connecticut troops, with two guns, under Stark's overall command, his right covered by the *fleches* and his left by the Mystic River.

Meanwhile, Putnam was being prevented from building more defences on Bunker's Hill by the hordes of deserters, stragglers and the genuinely bemused, whom he had neither the authority nor the skill to organize. Nevertheless, some men were still drifting forwards, including Major Generals Warren and Pomeroy, who offered their services to Prescott and Stark, respectively, as 'volunteers'.

By now, Howe had organised his force into two divisions, with the heavy guns remaining on the hill and the lighter 6-pdrs advancing with the infantry. Despite a growing suspicion that he was outnumbered, Howe knew he must clear the peninsula by dusk and time was short, leaving no alternative but to mount a frontal assault. He would lead the right division against the rail fence, whilst Pigott, on the left, would attack Charlestown and the redoubt to pin down their garrisons. As Pigott's men deployed, marksmen in Charlestown opened fire and Howe ordered the town to be burned – by 1600, it was blazing fiercely.

Leaving the remainder of Pigott's force to come ashore, Howe then advanced. The light infantry (unaware of Stark's wall) moved in fours along the beach to outflank the rail fence; four light 6pdrs, protected by the 35th's grenadiers, went ahead to destroy the rail fence and provide an opening for the grenadier battalion (led by Howe in person), followed by the 5th and 52nd, to roll up the position from north to south.

Clark's light battalion, led by his own regiment, the 23rd, reached Stark's marker and the defenders' front rank fired. Unable to deploy, the 4th and 10th struggled on, but were also shot down and the light battalion retreated, leaving 96 casualties on the beach.

It was only half a mile to the rail fence, but there were frequent halts to fire and negotiate obstacles and rough ground (which may have forced the artillery to veer away to the left). As the infantry approached the rail fence, it became clear that assigning the pioneers to Lieutenant Colonel Cleveland – who had stayed in Boston – had been a mistake. The grenadiers, in company columns, were climbing a fence some 90 yards from Knowlton, when they came under a premature fire and immediately

MAJOR GENERAL WILLIAM HOWE

RIGHT WING
Major General Howe

Light Infantry
Lieutenant Colonel Clark, 23rd Foot
(about 350 all ranks)[1]
23rd, 4th, 10th, 43rd, 52nd, 65th,
59th, 47th, 38th, 5th Foot

Grenadiers
Lieutenant Colonel James Abercrombie
(about 350 all ranks)
4th, 10th, 23rd, 43rd, 52nd, 59th,
47th, 38th, 18th/65th, 5th Foot

Artillery
Lieutenant Colonel Samuel Cleveland
(Boston) (about 350 all ranks)[2] Four 6-
pdrs, four 12-pdrs, four howitzers
Grenadier company 35th Foot[3]

Reserve
(about 500 all ranks)[4]
Battalion companies of the 5th and
52nd Foot

LEFT WING
Brigadier General Robert Pigott

II Brigade
Brigadier General Pigott
(about 750 all ranks)
Battalion companies of the 38th and
43rd Foot Flank companies of the 35th,
2nd Marines, 63rd Foot

Reserve
Major Thomas Pitcairn, Marines
(about 400 all ranks)
Battalion companies of the 47th Foot,
1st Marines

THIRD WAVE
Major General Henry Clinton
(about 800 all ranks)

Battalion companies of the 2nd
Marines, 63rd Foot

TOTAL STRENGTH
approximately 3500 with 12 guns[5]

Notes:
1. Strengths are approximate, based on the most recent returns available.
2. Includes 250 infantry detached to help move the guns and the 35th's grenadier company for protection.
3. The 35th, 49th and 63rd had just reached Boston, but only the 63rd and the 35th's flank companies had yet disembarked (all three regiments were at the new war establishment of 640 all ranks).
4. The battalion companies of each regiment were minus detachments assisting the artillery, a guard of 24 ranks (effectively a company) left in Boston to protect the camps, and losses from 19 April (offset by drafts of new recruits – about 40 per regiment – who had been assigned only the day before, and whose value can only be imagined).
5. The figure traditionally given by historians is 2500, but this must exclude officers and sergeants (British returns were unique in listing only the number of rank-and-file, i.e. the fire-power available); the 2nd Marines and 63rd Foot must also be excluded, as they arrived too late to take part in the fighting.

THE ROYAL NAVY

VESSELS	GUNS	POSITION ON 17 JUNE
Boyne	70	Harbour (not engaged)
Somerset	64	North Wharf (not engaged)
Preston	50	Harbour (not engaged)
Tartar	28	Harbour (guard ship)
Glasgow	20[1]	Opposite Charlestown cemetery
Lively	20[1]	Between Copps Hill and Charlestown
Falcon	14[2]	East of Breed's Hill
Spitfire	6[3]	Used as a tender
Symmetry	18[4]	Opposite Mill Dam
Gondolas	2[5]	Opposite Mill Dam

Notes:
(1) 9-pdrs as main armament
(2) 6-pdrs as main armament
(3) 3-pdrs as main armament
(4) 9-pdrs as main armament (Army vessel with Royal Navy crew and gunners)
(5) 12-pdrs as main armament (Army vessel with Royal Navy crew/Army gunners)

returned it. Eventually, the 5th and 52nd caught them up and as they crowded together, the attack lost its momentum and the regulars pulled back out of range to reform.

Howe rethought his plan; although he knew the beach was defended, this was still the vulnerable flank. Bringing the light infantry in to attack the rail fence, he ordered closer support from the artillery while he attacked the *fleches*. After a short break, he advanced again, but the attack

CAMBRIDGE

Major General Artemas Ward[1]

Artemas Ward[2] (1st Mass)	449
Asa Whitcomb (5th Mass)	399
John Mansfield (7th Mass)	345
William Prescott (9th Mass)	483
James Frye (10th Mass)	556
Ebenezer Bridge (11th Mass)	315 (6 Cos)
John Paterson (12th Mass)	524
James Scammon (13th Mass)	547
Thomas Gardner (15th Mass)	425
John Nixon (16th Mass)	224
Ephraim Doolittle (18th Mass)	308 (6 Cos)
Jonathan Brewer (19th Mass)	371 (8 Cos)
Benjamin Woodbridge (22nd Mass)	354
Moses Little (24th Mass)	509
Samuel Gerrish (25th Mass)	595
John Stark (1st NH)	823 (13 Cos)
James Reed (3rd NH)	534 (8 Cos)
Paul Sargent[3] (NH unattached)	220 (2 Cos)
Joseph Spencer[4] (2nd Conn)	1046
Israel Putnam (3rd Conn)	1046
Samuel Parsons (6th Conn)	210 (2 Cos)

ROXBURY

Major General John Thomas[5]

John Thomas (2nd Mass)	596
Timothy Walker (3rd Mass)	562
Theophilus Cotton (4th Mass)	?
Joseph Read (6th Mass)	594
Timothy Danielson (8th Mass)	? (8 Cos)
Ebenezer Learned (14th Mass)	?
John Fellows (17th Mass)	548
David Brewer (20th Mass)	350 (9 Cos)
William Heath (21st Mass)	545
Richard Gridley[6] (Artillery)	120 (3 Cos)
Thomas Church (1st RI)	500 (8 Cos)
Daniel Hitchcock (2nd RI)	500 (8 Cos)
James Varnum (3rd RI)	400 (7 Cos)[7]

Notes:
1. Total on 9 June, 7644, excluding officers.
2. Regiments were numbered according to the seniority of the counties the men came from (Woodbridge's, Little's were numbered after 17 June).
3. Originally in Massachusetts service discharged into New Hampshire service on 9 June.
4. About one-third of Spencer's men were with Thomas.
5. Massachusetts troops: about 4700 in 93 companies.
6. Richard Gridley's artillery regiment of 370 men was split two to one between Cambridge and Roxbury.
7. The eighth company was artillery (not included).

was a disaster, receiving a continued stream of fire for nearly 30 minutes. Many officers were shot down and some flank companies were reduced to single figures. The artillery support never materialised as the 6-pdrs had 12-pdr ammunition, for some unknown reason. The British tried to fire back, but did little damage and withdrew again, followed by Howe whose 12-man staff were all dead or wounded.

Once again, Howe had to reassess the overall position. More Americans were massing on Bunker's Hill – some were moving forward, others were building defensive works – and not only would he soon be unable to dislodge them, but they would accumulate sufficient strength to drive him back into the harbour. He ordered Clinton to send over reinforcements and reorganised for another assault.

Meanwhile, on the left, Pigott's force had made a feint against the redoubt, opening fire at extreme range, doing little damage but encouraging Prescott's men to use up some precious ammunition. As the 47th and 1st Marines moved around the south flank, Pigott advanced against the redoubt and breastwork. Prescott ordered his men to hold their fire until the British were within 30 yards – this action supposedly gave rise to the absurd order, 'Don't fire 'till you see the whites of their eyes'.

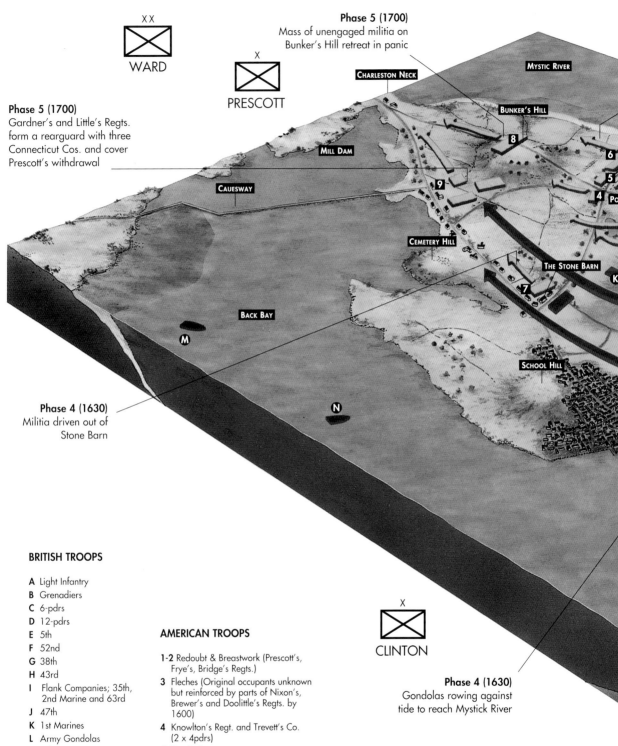

Phase 5 (1700)
Mass of unengaged militia on
Bunker's Hill retreat in panic

Phase 5 (1700)
Gardner's and Little's Regts.
form a rearguard with three
Connecticut Cos. and cover
Prescott's withdrawal

X X
WARD

X
PRESCOTT

MYSTIC RIVER

CHARLESTON NECK

BUNKER'S HILL

8

6

MILL DAM

5

4

PO

9

CAUESWAY

CEMETERY HILL

THE STONE BARN

K

7

BACK BAY

M

SCHOOL HILL

N

Phase 4 (1630)
Militia driven out of
Stone Barn

BRITISH TROOPS

A Light Infantry
B Grenadiers
C 6-pdrs
D 12-pdrs
E 5th
F 52nd
G 38th
H 43rd
I Flank Companies; 35th,
   2nd Marine and 63rd
J 47th
K 1st Marines
L Army Gondolas
M *Glasgow*
N *Symmetry*
O *Lively*
P *Falcon*
Q *Spitfire*
R Copp's Hill Battery
S 2nd Marines
T 63rd Foot

AMERICAN TROOPS

1-2 Redoubt & Breastwork (Prescott's,
     Frye's, Bridge's Regts.)
3 Fleches (Original occupants unknown
   but reinforced by parts of Nixon's,
   Brewer's and Doolittle's Regts. by
   1600)
4 Knowlton's Regt. and Trevett's Co.
   (2 x 4pdrs)
5 Reed's Regt.
6 Stark's Regt.
7 Stone Barn (Putman's Little's
   Doolittle's Woodbridge's –
   detachments of each)
8 Bunker's Hill (Putman with various
   Massachusetts contingents)
9 Rearguard (Little's, Gardner's and 3
   Connecticut Cos.)

X
CLINTON

Phase 4 (1630)
Gondolas rowing against
tide to reach Mystick River

Phase 5
Stark's command covers the retreat of Prescott's men and then retires in good order taking Trevett's remaining gun

Phase 4 (1630)
Light infantry engage Stark's men keeping them occupied during the final assualt

Phase 4 (1630)
Grenadiers and 5th Foot attack the *fleches* and the breastwork

Phase 4 (1630)
6-pdrs advance, their right protected by the light infantry, and enfilade the breastwork from flank

Phase 4 (1630)
52nd storms the breastwork

Phase 4 (1630)
Pigot's battalions storm the redoubt from three sides

STONE WALL

RAIL FENCE

A

THREE FLECHES

B

E

MARSHY GROUND

C

BRICK KILNS

D

MOULTON'S HILL

MOULTON'S POINT

3

2

F

1

SAND BANKS

G

H

BREED'S HILL

I

S

T

SECONDARY LANDINGS

Q

P

O

CHARLESTOWN

Phase 5 (1700)
Pigott's flank companies pursue Prescott's command, but run up against American rearguard

Phase 4 (1630)
Clinton arrives with the 2nd Marines and the 63rd and advances towards Charlestown Neck

L

BOSTON HARBOUR

R

HOWE

N

BATTLE OF BREED'S HILL
17 June 1775, 1600-1800, viewed from south-east showing the third British attack

Then they unleashed a volley that forced the regulars back out of range to regroup. The flanking party also withdrew, after running into some Massachusetts detachments driven out of Charlestown by the fires, and who had fortified a stone barn and surrounding farmyard.

THE FINAL ASSAULT

Spectators in Boston (including Clinton and Burgoyne) saw both British divisions recoil, and the crowds of wounded retiring to Moulton's Point. Clinton, responding to Howe's request, collected the 63rd and 2nd Marines and, asking Burgoyne to excuse him to Gage for leaving his post, followed them. Arriving at the beach (with several men in the boat already wounded by enemy fire), he formed the beach guard and walking wounded into an *ad hoc* unit and advanced.

Meanwhile, Howe had not been idle, sending companies of the 47th and 1st Marines to clear the marksmen from the outskirts of Charlestown and capture the stone barn. As the regulars formed up once more, the defenders at the rail fence discovered they had few rounds left and began rifling the pockets and cartridge boxes of the dead. In the redoubt, Prescott broke open the cartridges of the two abandoned cannon and shared out the coarse powder. No food, water or ammunition had come forward since they had arrived the previous night. In Cambridge, Ward was desperately trying to get supplies forward, but could not find anyone willing to take the wagons over the Neck, much less to Breed's Hill – those supplies that did get forward were consumed by the troops on Bunker's Hill.

By now, Ward had committed every man and gun; if Gage attacked across Boston Neck, he had nothing left to support Thomas, whose men were feverishly erecting barricades in Roxbury. In fact, Gage was unlikely to do any such thing, as aside from the light dragoons, who were still recovering from their sea voyage, his only reserves were Percy's brigade (which had replaced its loses of 19 April with raw recruits only the previous day). They which bombarded Roxbury from the defences on Boston Neck throughout the afternoon.

The men Ward had sent forward had still not arrived and several colonels would later face courts-martial charged with conduct ranging from mere dilatoriness to outright cowardice, as a result (in their defence, Ward had no trained staff and there were no maps of the area – those who had never been to Charlestown before may literally have got lost). On Bunker's Hill, stray shots had claimed the occasional victim throughout the afternoon, further demoralising the troops already there. Putnam, unable to control the men around him with orders, turned to curses and the flat of his sword, but to no effect; only a few of the better junior officers managed to lead small groups forward, mainly to the *fleches* which were the nearest defences to Bunker's Hill.

Howe had a new plan: the surviving light infantry (about 150 men) would engage the defenders of the rail fence, while the 6-pdrs would advance, their right protected by the light infantry, and enfilade the breastwork. At the same time, the 5th would attack the *fleches* and the grenadiers and 52nd the northern half of the breastwork, while Pigott's right (38th and 43rd) attacked the southern half and the front of the redoubt. The 47th and 1st Marines would sweep between Charlestown and the redoubt to attack its south and west faces. Once in possession of Breed's Hill, Howe could face any counter-attacks, or advance on Bunker's Hill, as he wished.

The 6-pdrs now had the correct ammunition and the end was nasty, brutish and short, as they swept the breastwork of defenders, who either fled or retired into the redoubt. The same happened at the *fleches*, and now it was the turn of American officers to be shot down trying to inspire their men. At the rail fence, Stark knew he had to cover Prescott's retreat, but also that he could very easily be cut off; he may have considered a counterattack against the weakened light companies, but he would have to cross the same disordering terrain as his opponents with men who were no match for the regulars at manoeuvring in the open.

Meanwhile, Prescott's men held their fire until the regulars were 20 yards away, then unleashed a devastating volley. But the regulars stormed into the ditch, and for a brief period neither side dared show itself over the top of the parapet. At the same time, the breastwork fell, its captors immediately coming under a brief, but stinging, crossfire from the *fleches* and the north face of the redoubt. Then three captains of the 52nd scaled the parapet of the breastwork; they were shot down, but their men burst over behind them, bayonetting the defenders.

To the south, the Marines had become disordered, crossing hedges and fences, and had lost several officers, including Major Pitcairn (wounded for the third time). The adjutant, Lieutenant Waller, reformed two companies and stopped the men firing, as the 47th formed on his left; together, the two battalions swarmed over the ditch and into the redoubt – probably the first troops to enter. Prescott ordered his men to retire through the gorge at the rear face (some of them had to find it with their hands, the smoke was so thick), as the regulars overwhelmed them and sent volleys crashing into their backs, killing Dr Warren. Seeing Prescott fall back, Stark also retired, taking Trevett's remaining gun, after a tussle with men of the 5th.

Although the reserves on Bunker's Hill outnumbered Howe on their own, panic took over as the battle they had avoided all afternoon came inexorably nearer. Clinton arrived at the redoubt and took over the pursuit from the weary Howe. Pausing to leave 100 of his *ad hoc* unit from the beach in the redoubt, thus providing a rallying point if anything should go wrong, he prepared to attack Bunker's Hill. Ahead of him, amidst the fleeing masses, were small groups heroically trying to cover the retreat. One such group consisted of Gardner's and Little's regiments, with three Connecticut companies; they formed up behind a low, thin, stone wall and traded volleys for several minutes with Pigott's three light companies, before withdrawing, fence by fence, to the Neck, leaving the regulars with heavy losses (the 35th's light company was reduced to five men).

All this time, fresh American regiments were still arriving, but even those keen to get forward could hardly pass the hordes streaming in the opposite direction, as the *Glasgow* and *Symmetry* pounded the Neck. Putnam finally accepted defeat and rode away, carrying valuable entrenching tools (probably the only ones saved that day). As the regulars reached

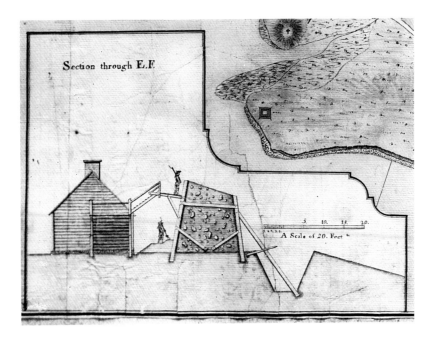

Section through E.F.

A Scale of 20. Feet

Fortification on Bunker's Hill. Montresor followed his father as senior engineer in North America, but often, officers were appointed merely on the basis of an ability to draw. After the action on 17 June, he began the construction of defensive works to prevent the Rebels ocupying the Neck and this is a section through the citadel, which included a moat (ditch) and drawbridge, guardhouses and gun emplacements. (William L Clements Library, University of Michigan)

the Neck, Howe ordered Clinton to halt, as his force was too depleted, especially in officers, to carry on, and the reinforcements (2nd Marines and 63rd) had not yet caught up. Fortified posts were set up to cover the road and the north end of the Mill Dam, and secure the peninsula; it was still only 1700.

Unshaken by the chaos around him, Ward had his remaining Connecticut units cover the retreat and later, Putnam had them build another fort on Winter Hill, west of the Neck. They kept up a sporadic fire from some houses throughout the evening, until Howe brought up a 12-pdr and the *Glasgow* bombarded groups of Americans near the neck. Clinton's advance had also trapped a number of them in copses and empty houses all over the peninsula, and mopping up continued for several days.

Meanwhile, back to the east the *Somerset* had landed water for the troops, while boats ferried the injured back over to Boston – among them Pitcairn and Abercrombie, both mortally wounded, and Captain Harris of the 5th's grenadier company, who would watch, with the aid of mirrors, as the surgeon operated on his exposed brain. Many men had severe leg wounds that would lead to amputation or death from gangrene, following their opponents' use of scrap metal and nails, instead of ball ammunition.

In 90 minutes, and in an area less than half a mile square, the regulars lost 226 dead and over 900 wounded – almost half those engaged (the oft-quoted figure of 1054 casualties excludes an unknown number of wounded from the 38th, which had the most dead of any regular unit). The losses in officers, 19 dead and 70 wounded, were particularly severe and would represent one-quarter of all British officer casualties in the Revolution. The Americans lost between 400 and 600, mostly in the retreat; Massachusetts lost 115 dead, 305 wounded and 30 captured (mostly wounded), while Stark reported 19 dead and 74 wounded from his and

Reed's regiments (Knowlton's losses are unrecorded, but were probably negligible). In one category, though, their losses heavily outweighed those of the regulars – hundreds of men simply went home during and after the battle. The various provincial governments took prompt steps to return many of them, but for the moment, their absence added to Ward's already dangerous weakness.

On 18 June, Howe burned the houses west of the Neck to protect his working parties on Bunker's Hill from sniping. Meanwhile, Clinton urged Gage to go ahead with the plan to occupy Dorchester Heights, while the opposition was still weak (in fact, Ward had just taken 1000 men from Thomas to strengthen his own left). But Gage did nothing until 24 June, when three gondolas and the 2nd Marines, 63rd and the 64th's flank companies were detailed to storm the Heights, in concert with a diversionary attack from Charlestown peninsula and an artillery bombardment of Roxbury from Boston Neck.

As ever, word got out and Gage called off the attack at the last moment (the bombardment of Roxbury went ahead, but did no damage). Ward had indeed learned of the operation and reinforced Thomas, but the latter had still not fortified the heights and would have ended up having to fight the regulars in the open, in order to oppose the landing.

Instead, Howe established a permanent camp on Charlestown peninsula, as both Gage and the Provincial Congress sent despatches to London giving their own versions of a battle fought between two raw and inexperienced armies, and won by superior leadership and discipline, but at a crippling cost in human life.

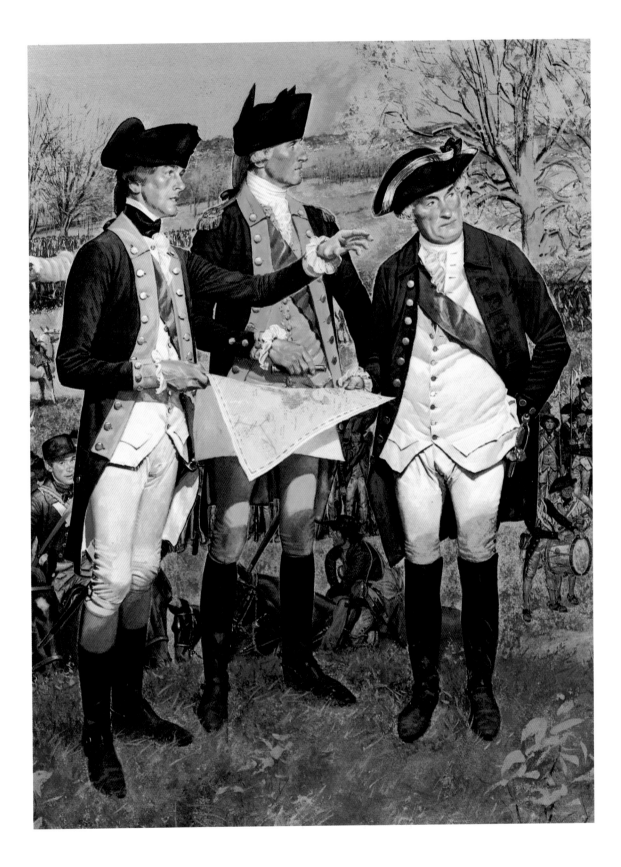

THE SIEGE

WASHINGTON TAKES COMMAND

On 3 July, General George Washington arrived in Cambridge to take over from Ward. Though there were no further set-piece battles, the following months saw continuous activity, especially on the Boston and Charlestown necks, as Washington and his junior officers attempted to organise the various American contingents into something resembling an army.

On 21 July, an American detachment raided Nantasket Point to collect fodder, then crossed to Great Brewster Island, where they removed lamps, oil and gunpowder from the lighthouse, and burnt its wooden parts. Ten days later, 33 Marines and 10 workmen sent to repair the lighthouse were killed or captured by 300 men in whaleboats.

During the night of 26 August, a 1200-man working party with 2400 guards built a fort on Ploughed Hill, a low eminence on the Charlestown-Medford road. It was bombarded the next day from Bunker's Hill, and a ship and two floating batteries in the Back Bay. British troops were seen forming up on the peninsula and Washington summoned 5000 men, but nothing further happened.

As autumn became winter, the British suffered shortages of food, clothing and firewood (every wooden building in Boston had gone by the end of the siege), while the Americans lacked warm winter quarters and many drifted away until the British outnumbered Washington's besiegers. Meanwhile, Gage had been summoned home in September, and probably suspected the reception that awaited him, as he had shown no ability to shape events, preferring to wait and then react to them. Howe received the local rank of General and as a result became *de facto* commander in chief of the King's troops in North America. He wanted to quit Boston immediately, but was prevented from doing so by lack of ships and the worsening weather.

Largely as a result of these conditions that British foraging raids became more common: nine companies of light infantry and 100 grenadiers seized ten cows in a raid on Lechmere Point on 9 November, after a skirmish with the Pennsylvania riflemen and two Massachusetts regiments. In response,

Washington and Ward survey Boston's defences. A modern work by Charles McBarron, it accurately portrays the lack of uniformity of the New England Army units, seen behind Washington (centre) and Ward (right). It is interesting to note the use of pole arms by company officers and NCOs – weapons normally associated only with the British forces (and, later, their German allies). (Courtesy, Army Art Collection, West Point, New York)

A panorama of Boston and its environs. A panoramic view from Beacon Hill, done in the autumn of 1775 by Lieutenants Williams and Woode of the 23rd Foot, in five parts, of which four are reproduced; the fifth shows the islands to the north east of Boston. (All plates: Massachusetts Historical Society, Boston)

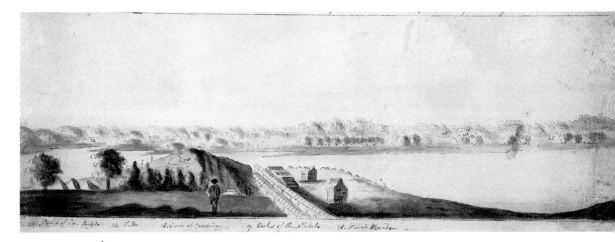

Rebel encampments and the town of Cambridge are just visible on the hills west of Boston. The huts in the foreground are ropewalks (also seen in the work showing Boston in 1764); to their left is the (in)famous Mount Whoredom.

In the middle distance are more Rebel defences and encampments, including a signalling post; a British ship is anchored in the Back Bay to prevent raids.

Putnam's men fortified Cobble Hill during the night two weeks later.

On 8 January, a force under Knowlton – now a major in the 20th Continental regiment – attacked Charlestown, burning the last houses and capturing five prisoners.*

*At the time, some British officers were performing a play by Burgoyne entitled 'The Blockade of Boston'; when a sergeant ran on stage to give the alarm, the audience cheered, thinking he was one of the cast!

From the left, Boston harbour and the South End, with Castle William visible to the right of the spire of the Old South Meeting House; Dorchester Neck is left centre. At centre is Boston Neck, with the Blockhouse half way along, and Boston Common, still in use as a military *camp, in the foreground. The large house in the right foreground belonged to John Hancock; Roxbury Meeting House can be seen immediately above it, with Rebel entrenchments and tents on the hillside to its right.*

In the right foreground is Boston's North End, with Charlestown peninsula to its right; the British lines on the Neck, their camp on Bunker Hill and the captured redoubt on Breed's Hill, can be seen above the burned ruins of Charlestown.

A NOBLE TRAIN OF ARTILLERY

By mid-January, a council of war agreed that Washington had to attack before further British reinforcements arrived in the spring, but this was difficult, as the Americans lacked the heavy artillery to support it. Some 87 siege pieces had been captured at Crown Point and Fort Ticonderoga the previous year and Colonel Henry Knox, commander of the newly-raised Continental Artillery regiment, proposed to bring them to Boston. Selecting

Looking south towards Roxbury, some of the minor defences can be seen along the western shoreline of the peninsula. The small fortified 'island' is called Fox Hill, and was completely accessible by land at low tide; the defensive work to its left is Powder House Hill. Moving north, the large redoubt is on West Hill, the westernmost peak of Beacon Hill. (Spencer Collection, New York Public Library)

BRITISH ARMY AT BOSTON, 1 January 1776

COMMANDER IN CHIEF [1]
GENERAL WILLIAM HOWE

GRENADIERS
Brigadier General Moncrieffe
1st Bn *Lieutenant Colonel Meadows*
4th, 5th, 10th, 17th, 22nd, 23rd, 27th, 35th, 38th, 40th [2]

2nd Bn *Lieutenant Colonel Monckton*
43rd, 44th, 45th, 49th, 52nd, 55th, 63rd, 64th, 1st and 2nd Marines

LIGHT INFANTRY
Brigadier General Leslie
1st Bn *Major Musgrave*
4th, 5th, 10th, 17th, 22nd, 23rd, 27th, 35th, 38th, 40th

2nd Bn *Major Maitland*
43rd, 44th, 45th, 49th, 52nd, 55th, 63rd, 64th, 1st and 2nd Marines

I Brigade *Major General Robinson:* 4th, 27th, 45th Foot

II Brigade *Major General Pigott:* 5th, 35th, 49th Foot

III Brigade *Major General Jones:* 10th, 38th, 52nd Foot

IV Brigade *Major General Grant:* 17th, 40th, 55th Foot

V Brigade *Major General Smith:* 22nd, 43rd, 63rd Foot

VI Brigade *Major General Agnew:* 23rd, 44th, 64th Foot

Unbrigaded 17th Light Dragoons, 1st and 2nd Marines

Notes:
1. Local rank only; within the Army, he remained a major general.
2. The 18th and 59th Foot were drafted as replacements within the garrison, while the officers, NCOs and musicians returned to England; the companies of the 65th Foot returned to Halifax; and the 47th Foot was sent to Canada to repel the American invasion.

60 guns and mortars (three of which weighed over a ton each), he transported them 350 miles over inhospitable terrain in mid-winter, arriving in Cambridge on 25 January.

On 16 February, Washington proposed an attack across the ice-covered Back Bay, estimating his own strength at 16,000 and the British at 5000, but his officers considered these figures too optimistic, and, in any event,

the assault would need several days' preliminary bombardment at least.

Their counter-proposal was to seize Dorchester Heights, which, with Knox's guns, would give the Americans command of Boston harbour and force the British to attack across Boston Neck. The works would have to be completed in one night, and as the ground was frozen, digging would be impossible, so the defences were built in pre-fabricated sections, with fitted gabions, fascines, barrels of earth to roll down on any attackers, and abattis from the nearby orchards. Putnam, with 4000 men, 45 boats and two floating batteries, was ready to counter-attack across the Back Bay should the British appear.

THE SIEGE OF BOSTON, JULY 1775 TO MARCH 1776

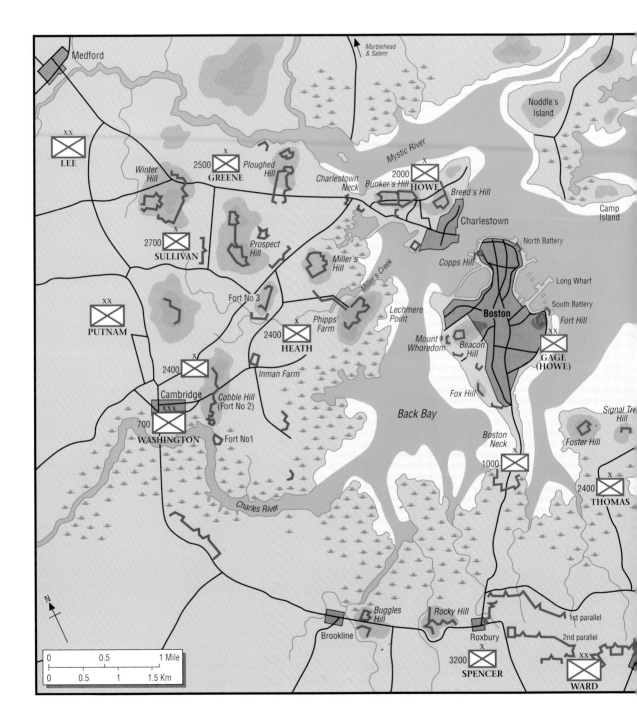

Medford

Marblehead & Salem

Noddle's Island

XX
LEE

2500 X GREENE

Ploughed Hill

Winter Hill

Mystic River

Charlestown Neck

Bunker's Hill

2000 X HOWE

Breed's Hill

Camp Island

Charlestown

2700 X SULLIVAN

Prospect Hill

Miller's Hill

Miller's Creek

North Battery

Copps Hill

Long Wharf

Fort No 3

Lechmere Point

South Battery

Fort Hill

XX
PUTNAM

2400 X HEATH

Phipps Farm

Mount Whoredom

Beacon Hill

Boston

XX
GAGE (HOWE)

2400 X

Inman Farm

Fox Hill

2400 X

700 XXX WASHINGTON

Cambridge

Cobble Hill (Fort No 2)

Fort No1

Back Bay

Boston Neck

Signal Tre Hill

Foster Hill

1000 X

2400 X THOMAS

Charles River

Buggles Hill

Rocky Hill

1st parallel

Brookline

Roxbury

2nd parallel

3200 X SPENCER

XX
WARD

N

| 0 | 0.5 | 1 Mile |
| 0 | 0.5 1 | 1.5 Km |

The panorama of Boston beginning on p.72 and continued here was executed by Lieutenant Archibald Robertson, an engineer officer, during February 1776, and it is interesting to compare it with the Williams panorama, to see how the siege and the changing seasons had altered the area. (Spencer Collection, New York Public Library)

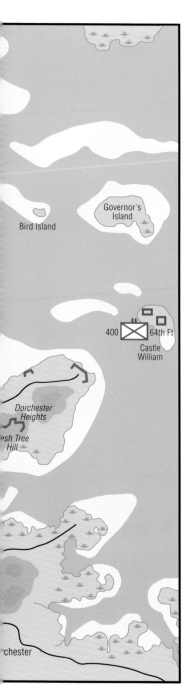

These two views show (above) the northwest of Boston peninsula, with Charlestown peninsula in the left middle distance (once again, note how prominent School Hill is among the ruins of Charlestown, with Breed's Hill immediately behind it). The masts of the ships in the harbour can be seen above the rooftops of the North End, and the Old North Meeting House can be seen just beyond the mill dam, in the left centre. In the lower view looking east, Dorchester Neck can be seen beyond the South End of Boston, with the Common at the bottom right corner. The house with four chimneys is probably John Hancock's, and just to its left is Beacon Hill.

COMMANDER-IN-CHIEF
GENERAL GEORGE WASHINGTON

Headquarters troops:

Continental Rifle Regiment[2]	–	372/504
United Colonies Artillery Regt[3]	–	519/555

Major General Ward's Division (Boston Neck)

Brigadier General Thomas

1st Mass Regt Ward	449	408/512
2nd Mass Regt Thomas	500	412/543
4th Mass Regt Cotton	500	418/548
8th Mass Regt Danielson	493	484/574
17th Mass Regt Fellows	434	417/539
20th Mass Regt D Brewer	374	351/460

Brigadier General Spencer

2nd Conn Regt Spencer }	2333[4]	189/296[5]
6th Conn Regt Parson }		177/182
8th Conn Regt ?	–[6]	140/164
3rd Mass Regt Walker	491	406/486
6th Mass Regt Read	523	414/529
14th Mass Regt Learned	489	391/459
Md & Va Rifle Cos Four	–	244/280
Independent Cos Six	239[7]	49/449

Major General Lee's Division (Charlestown)

Brigadier General Sullivan

1st NH Regt Stark }		341/58[7]
2nd NH Regt Poor }	1664	367/534
3rd NH Regt Reed		389/504
7th Conn Regt ?	–	–/–[8]
7th Mass Regt Mansfield	490	338/609
16th Mass Regt Nixon	489	346/498
18th Mass Regt Doolittle	393	327/448

Brigadier General Greene

1st RI Regt Varnum		369/482
2nd RI Regt Hitchcock }	1085	317/445
3rd RI Regt Church		285/406
15th Mass Regt Gardner	417	309/496
19th Mass Regt J Brewer	301	315/417
24th Mass Regt Little	472	349/564

Major General Putnam's Division (Cambridge)

Brigadier General Heath:

5th Mass Regt Whitcomb	523	411/587
9th Mass Regt Prescott	430	407/493
12th Mass Regt Paterson	409	416/539
13th Mass Regt Scammon	456	463/550
21st Mass Regt Heath	483	422/558
25th Mass Regt Gerrish	498	557/632
26th Mass Regt Phinney	319	427/519

Brigadier General (Vacant)

3rd Conn Regt Putnam	–[4]	82/154
10th Mass Regt Frye	406	384/535
11th Mass Regt Bridge	470	360/533
22nd Mass Regt Woodbridge	366	302/506
23rd Mass Regt Glover	454	229/547[9]
27th Mass Regt Sargent	–[10]	358/483

Notes:
1. Returns are for 19 July and 30 December.
2. Mixed unit from Pennsylvania, Maryland and Virginia; did not arrive until after 19 July.
3. Substantially Massachusetts companies, with New York and Rhode Island companies absorbed in November.
4. Includes Putnam's regiment (Vacant Brigade).
5. The Connecticut regiments' enlistments expired on 10 December; the figures in this column are those willing to re-enlist.
6. Did not arrive until August; both it and the 7th had the smaller 79-man companies from the start.
7. Only four companies on 19 July.
8. Did not arrive until August; left before December.
9. Part of this regiment was assigned to naval duties.
10. Originally commanded New Hampshire volunteers.

MAIN ARMY AT BOSTON, July – December 1776[1]

On the night of 4 March, Thomas moved 1200 men onto the heights in bright moonlight, but with a ground haze hiding them from British view. The sound of their work was hidden by a bombardment (digging noises were reported to Smith, but he did nothing), and by dawn the next day, they had almost completed the two small forts. Howe, informed that the harbour was now unsafe for ships and that his guns could not elevate sufficiently to hit the works, planned a night attack by 2200 men under Brigadier General Jones, but called it off at the last minute, citing bad weather – this decision later led to Graves being wrongly blamed for failing to give support.

The British defeated an attempt to extend the position onto Nook's Hill, four days later, but on 17 March 11,000 soldiers and sailors, with 1000 Loyalists, sailed out into Nantasket Roads. There they remained for five days before sailing for Halifax, in Nova Scotia, rather than New York, as expected – the last to leave was the 64th Foot, which blew up Castle William.

COMMANDER-IN-CHIEF

GENERAL GEORGE WASHINGTON

Headquarters troops:
1st Continental Regiment[2]
Continental Artillery, Colonel Henry Knox

Major General Ward's Division (Boston Neck)

Brigadier General Thomas:
3rd, 21st, 23rd Continental Regiments[3]

Brigadier General Spencer:
10th(Cn), 13th, 17th(Cn), 19th(Cn), 22nd(Cn) Continental Regiments
Independent rifle companies (2 Md, 1 Va)

Major General Lee's Division (Charlestown)

Brigadier General Sullivan:
2nd(NH), 4th, 5th(NH), 8th(NH) Continental Regiments
Brigadier General Greene:
6th, 9th(RI), 11th(RI), 12th, 25th Continental Regiments

Major General Putnam's Division (Cambridge)

Brigadier General Heath:
7th, 15th[4], 18th, 24th, 26th Continental Regiments

Vacant Brigade[5]:
14th, 16th, 20th(Cn), 27th Continental Regiments

Notes:
1. Effective strength by the end of February, 8212 enlisted men, with 5582 present and fit for duty; by March, 14,400, with 3000 sick (300 in hospital) and 1300 detached on duty elsewhere.
2. The rifle regiment, now all from Pennsylvania.
3. Continental Regiments are all former Massachusetts units, unless otherwise indicated.
4. Exchanged for 16th (Vacant Brigade) in February.
5. Commander Brigadier General Frye after 16 February.

Washington had agreed not to attack if Howe did not burn the town; as the British left, Ward entered with 500 men. The main body, marching in three days later, found 100 cannon (of which 69 were salvaged), stores, all the medical supplies and 3000 blankets, left behind by lack of ships and administrative errors. The last eight months of the siege cost Washington 20 dead.

The Revolution would be America's longest war, until Vietnam, but for Boston, where it had begun 11 months earlier, the war was already over.

AFTERMATH

REACTION IN GREAT BRITAIN AND EUROPE

The war soon became a talking point throughout Europe, as well as in Great Britain and North America (French agents had penetrated the Admiralty in London, and were aware of British plans and strengths – though not much information was yet being passed to the Americans).

Opinion in Parliament was divided, the Whigs welcoming American success and courting favour with their London agents, while the Tories predictably fulminated against the 'damned rebels'. Among the public, however, there was no outcry or patriotic demonstration – it was not their fight, after all. Recruiting, if anything, became harder, forcing the Government to look to Europe (as ever). Russia declined to supply troops and Prussia was positively hostile (Frederick the Great, still smarting over the supposed betrayal by 'perfidious Albion'), but a host of smaller German states – many very poor – saw a rare chance to fill the national coffers, and agreed to send men to America.

However, these forces would not be ready for several months and reinforcements were needed now. When word of the first clashes arrived, the Government was forced to place the Army on a war footing: every infantry regiment acquired two additional companies, to remain in England or Ireland as a depot and cadre, while light dragoon regiments added a cornet, a sergeant, two Corporals and 30 privates per troop. In Scotland, the former Jacobite Simon Fraser raised a two-battalion regiment (71st Foot), while the 60th (Royal Americans) was allowed to raise two more battalions in England and Hanover respectively.

Among senior officers, there was a drastic reappraisal of their opponents; at the end of June, Gage wrote that they displayed, 'a Spirit and Conduct against us they never showed against the French . . . everybody has Judged of them from their former appearance and behaviour'. Percy reported after Lexington, that 'the Rebels . . . are determined to go through with it, nor will the insurrection here turn out so despicable as it is perhaps imagined at home'. While Clinton remained sceptical of anything military in America, Howe was deeply affected by the events of 17 June – it is a moot point whether that experience, his Whig sympathies, or a secret

A Grenadier Company Officer of the 10th Foot. This unit was part of Smith's command at Lexington and at Breed's Hill attacked the rail fence with the rest of the Grenadier Battalion. (Gerry Embleton)

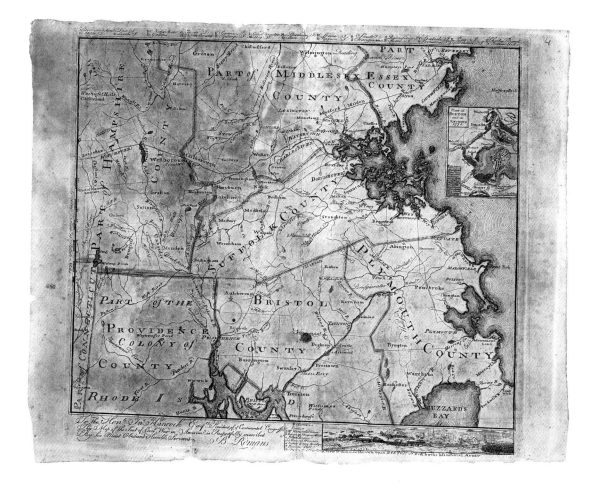

Map of the Seat of Civil War. Drawn for John Hancock, the President of the Continental Congress, the map defines the counties of Massachusetts around Boston, and also shows the East Anglian and West Country influences in the names. It is interesting to note that the corresponding areas in England were the seat of both the Civil War and, later, the Monmouth Rebellion. (Massachusetts Historical Society, Boston)

political assignment, was responsible for his lack of ruthlessness in subsequent campaigns.

THE AMERICAN VIEW

In the Colonies two problems had to be faced, however unpalatable to politicians. First, while the militia's 'patriotic amateur' status might make it politically acceptable, it alone could never defeat the King's 'paid hirelings'. Second, after the initial enthusiasm for the 'defence of liberty', the attraction of military life soon waned, especially for those who had left farms and workbenches unattended. The Colonies needed their own 'regulars', men without homes, jobs or families to distract them, governed by proper military discipline rather than the easy-going egalitarianism that had paralysed the regiments on Bunker's Hill. By the end of the war, Congress would control such an army.

In 1775, few people wanted war and even fewer sought independence; that it happened was the result of mistakes and misconceptions on both sides and cynical manipulation by a small group with vested interests.

Revolutionary myths still endure, but an interview in 1842 between the US historian, Mellen Chamberlain, and a survivor of the fight at Concord Bridge, Captain Preston (then 91) is enlightening. It went as follows;

C: 'Did you take up arms against intolerable oppressions?'

P: 'Oppressions? I didn't feel them.'

C: 'Were you not oppressed by the Stamp Act?'

P: 'I never saw one . . . (and) certainly never paid a penny for one of them.'

C: 'Well, what about the Tea Tax?'

P: 'I never drank a drop of the stuff!'

C: 'Then I suppose you had been reading . . . about the eternal principles of liberty?'

P: 'We read only The Bible, The Catechism, Watts' Psalms and Hymns, and the Almanac.'

C: 'Well then . . . what did you mean in going to the fight?'

P: 'What we meant . . . was this: we had always governed ourselves and we always meant to.'

THE BATTLEFIELDS TODAY

The two battlefields are tended by a combination of local historical societies and two national historical parks – Boston and Minuteman. Of the two battlefields, that of 19 April – 'Battle Road' – is the better preserved and accessible. Colonial Boston and Charlestown were both eaten up by urban development, and land reclamation – especially the levelling of the hills and infilling of the Back Bay – has left them virtually unrecognisable.

LEXINGTON AND CONCORD

For this section of the tour, a car is a necessity and it is important to remember that most of the buildings are private homes with no public access; also, the main road is very busy and it is better to park in one of the car parks, rather than stop or slow down on the road.

Subsequent development makes it virtually impossible to follow Smith's and Percy's exact routes out of Boston, and it is best to start at the Visitor Centre in Lexington. Cross the road to Battle Green, a triangular patch of

Buckman's Tavern, Lexington. The main part of the building dates from well before 1775, but the 'wings' are later extensions. The stables and outhouses shown in contemporary prints and engravings no longer exist. (Author's photograph)

grass formed by Massachusetts Avenue and Bedford Road (State Highway 4/225). At the south-east apex is a statue of Captain Parker and behind it are stones marking where the meeting house, the belfry and the school stood. To the north-east is another stone, where Parker's men formed their line on that fateful morning. Most of the original buildings – Buckman's Tavern (beside the Visitor Centre) and Nathan Munroe's and Jonathan Harrington's houses – still surround the Green; the Clarke house (from which Adams and Hancock were evacuated) has been moved from Bedford Street to Hancock Street.

From the Green, drive towards Concord along Massachusetts Avenue and about a mile and a half beyond the bridge over Interstate 95 is a small stone where Revere was captured. From there, follow North Great Road (State Highway 2A) and Lexington Road right into Concord (leave the remoter sections of Battle Road for the return journey) and turn left at Wright's Tavern (Smith's headquarters) down Main Street (also known as Mill Dam Road), which leads to South Bridge. Returning to the town centre, turn left just before the war memorial and head out on Monument Street to North Bridge car park, past the Jones house and the Old Manse.

Proceed on foot down the dirt track to the bridge (notice how much more heavily wooded the area is today), passing the British memorial* and, on the far side, the famous 'Minute Man' statue, by Daniel French.

Across North Bridge, the track turns right up to the Visitor Centre, past the height where the light companies watched the militia. Behind the Visitor Centre is Liberty Street, bounded by the stone walls constantly referred to by the British, Major Buttrick's house, and Punkatasset Hill. The Visitor Centre is very good and has a superb relief model of the whole area as it was on 19 April – the road Parsons took no longer exists, so those wishing to see Barrett's farm should leave the Centre and turn left off Liberty Street into Barnes Hill Road, continuing over the crossroads into Barrett's Mill Road.

*'They came three thousand miles and died, To keep the past upon the throne; Unheard, beyond the ocean tide, Their English mother made her moan.'

ABOVE *North Bridge, Concord (looking north). The original bridge was removed and not replaced until the centennial celebrations of 1875; the bridge in the photograph is the fifth 'replacement'. Compare the dense foliage surrounding the approaches to the bridge with the open fields shown in the Doolittle engraving. (Author's photograph)*

ABOVE RIGHT *Wright's Tavern, Concord. The inn appears much as it did on 19 April, when it was used by Smith and Pitcairn for their headquarters. To the left is the present meeting house, and the road to the right leads to the South Bridge along Main Street (sometimes called Mill Dam Street). (Author's photograph)*

Leaving Concord on Lexington Road, The Wayside, home of Concord's muster master, Samuel Whitney, is about three-quarters of a mile beyond Wright's Tavern. About 600 yards further on is Merriam's Corner, where there are two houses (the Merriam House is the one set back along the Old Bedford Road), but the small bridge no longer exists. From there, Battle Road continues past Hardy's Hill and on to the Bloody Angles (scene of several ambushes) and then turns left into Virginia Road, past the houses Dr Prescott called at, the Hartwell Tavern and, after rejoining the North Great Road, the house of William Smith, captain of the Lincoln minutemen.

Follow the signs to the Minuteman Visitor Centre, which has displays, a film show and two guided walks. One heads west for almost half a mile, past the remains of the two Nelson homes, and gives a good idea of the road surface in colonial times (though the countryside would have been more visible, with far fewer trees). The other tour goes east for over a mile, along Marrett Street, past The Bluff and round Fiske Hill, where Smith was wounded trying to rally his men.

The Park ends here, but the withdrawal continued back through Lexington, passing the Munroe Tavern (Percy's headquarters on 19 April) and then through Arlington (Menotomy), where Jason Russell's house and the Cooper Tavern can still be seen; continue through Somerville past Prospect and Winter hills to Charlestown Neck, along Washington Street and Cambridge Street. If time permits, visit Cambridge and Harvard, as both have many colonial period buildings such as the Wadsworth House, which was Washington's first headquarters.

BUNKER'S (BREED'S) HILL AND BOSTON

Traffic in Boston is notoriously heavy, and sightseeing is best done on foot, using Rapid Transit – the 'T' – for long distances (it even goes out as far as Lexington).

Not much of the battlefield remains, as Charlestown has merged into Cambridge and Somerville. The Bunker Hill Pavilion, next to the US Navy Yard in Constitution Road, has an entertaining 'light-and-sound' show of the events of June 1775, and provides a good starting point. From there, head north on Park Street to Winthrop Street and the Old Training Field (the Charlestown militia's muster field) and into Monument Square.

The statue of William Prescott, Bunker's Hill Memorial, faces the south side of the memorial park and stands in front of the obelisk. Prescott's great-grandson is believed to have modelled for the sculptor and Prescott is shown in the long coat and floppy hat he wore on 17 June. (Author's photograph)

The Bunker Hill Monument is a landscaped, four-acre site in a residential area and all that remains of Breed's Hill. The four gates (commemorating the United States, Massachusetts, New Hampshire and Connecticut) lead to a 221-feet high obelisk, flanked by a small museum and a statue of Colonel Prescott.

The hollow obelisk is set roughly on the south-east corner of the redoubt and the area around it is where Pigott's flank companies and the Marines and 47th would have attacked. The small museum next door contains the entrance to the obelisk's staircase and also several dioramas, busts and paintings. Every 17 June, Bostonians in period uniforms conduct a mock battle on the site, which also contains plaques indicating various important features. On a hot summer's day, the slopes of the site and the surrounding streets give an idea of what Pigott's men faced on 17 June.

During the siege, artillery fire and shortages of firewood ensured that few ordinary buildings survived in Boston itself. However, several important edifices were restored or rebuilt and can be found on the 'Freedom Trail' (a red painted line, or red stones, along the pavement).

From Breed's Hill, cross Charlestown Bridge to Copp's Hill burial ground (next to the site of the battery) and the Old North Church, then south to Paul Revere's house in Garden Court. Beyond Interstate 93 is Faneuil Hall (rebuilt in the colonial style, but with an extra floor), while across Congress Street is the Old State House, now a museum and home to the Bostonian Society, and the site of the Boston Massacre, marked by a ring of cobbles in the road. Finally, head south on Washington Street to the Old South Meeting House, fully restored and with a model of colonial Boston.

Other places worth visiting are the King's Chapel, used by Loyalists during the siege, and the Old Granary Burial Ground, where Joseph Warren and Paul Revere are interred. The Trail ends on the Common, smaller than in colonial times, but similar in character.

Dorchester Heights can be reached by going south on Congress Street and over the bridge into South Boston, turning right into A Street, left onto Broadway, then right at G Street. On the left, in Thomas Park, is a monument resembling the spire of a colonial meeting house, commemorating the events of March 1776. From the tower, the commanding view of Boston and the harbour shows why the British were forced to evacuate.

Finally, a modern site worth visiting is the John Hancock Observatory in Copley Square (actually in the Back Bay), which has panoramic views and a 'light-and-sound' show of colonial Boston and the events of 1775.

Both Minuteman and Boston National Historical Parks provide detailed scale maps and information leaflets which, combined with a standard Boston street guide, allow all these places to be easily located and visited.

CHRONOLOGY

EVENTS LEADING UP TO THE BATTLE OF LEXINGTON AND CONCORD

10 February 1763 – Treaty of Paris signed

7 October 1763 – Proclamation of 1763

22 March 1765 – Stamp Act

7 October 1765 – Stamp Act Congress in New York

18 March 1766 – Repeal of the Stamp Act

29 June 1767 – The Townshend Acts

5 March 1770 – The Boston 'Massacre'

12 April 1770 – Repeal of Townshend Acts (except tea)

9 June 1772 – The *Gaspee* affair

10 May 1773 – Tea Act

16 December 1773 – The Boston 'tea party'

31 March 1774 – Passing of the first of the Intolerable (Coercive) Acts

1 June 1774 – Boston port closed

1 September 1774 – Gage seizes military stores

5 September 1774 – First Continental Congress

17 September 1774 – The Suffolk Resolves

4 December 1774 – New Hampshire militia capture guns from Fort William and Mary, Portsmouth

16 December 1774 – Rhode Island militia capture 44 guns from Fort George, Newport

16 January 1775 – Brown and de Berniere explore Worcester and Suffolk

26 February 1775 – Salem bridge affair

20 March 1775 – Brown and de Berniere reconnoitre Concord

30 March 1775 – Percy's brigade marches to Jamaica Plain

8 April 1775 – Prominent opposition leaders leave Boston

15 April 1775 – Gage takes flank companies off normal duties; Committee of Safety is warned

18-19 APRIL LEXINGTON AND CONCORD

0900 – Cannon moved from Concord to Groton

1700 – British patrols ride into the countryside

2000 – Mitchell's patrol passes through Lexington

2200 – Flank companies assembled on Boston Common

2300 – Revere rowed across to Charlestown

0030 – Forced away from Cambridge to Medford, Revere arrives in Lexington, followed soon after by Dawes

0130 – Revere captured by Mitchell's patrol

0200 – Smith's column leaves Lechmere Point; Dr Prescott alerts the militia in Concord

0230 – Mitchell heads for Menotomy and releases Revere

0430 – Parker's scout reports Smith half-a-mile away and his 'minute men' reassemble on Lexington Common

0500 – Pitcairn orders Parker's men to disperse; first shots and casualties of the American Revolution

0700 – Smith's column arrives in Concord; Parsons and Pole despatched to North and South bridges

0900 – Percy's brigade leaves Boston (having waited five hours for the Marines to assemble)

0930 – Fighting begins at North Bridge

1100 – Parsons returns safely to Concord

1200 – Smith orders his men to return to Boston

1230 – Exchange of fire at Merriam's Corner

1330 – Smith's column enters the 'Bloody Angles'

1430 – Smith wounded attempting to rally his men at Fiske Hill

1500 – Smith's column reaches Percy's brigade, half-a-mile east of Lexington

1530 – Percy starts withdrawal to Boston

1630 – British reach Menotomy, scene of the day's bloodiest fighting

1800 – Percy decides to march to Charlestown, rather than back through Cambridge

1900 – The British reach Charlestown peninsula

EVENTS LEADING UP TO THE BATTLE OF BREED'S HILL:

20 April 1775 – 20,000 to 30,000 militia surround Boston

10 May 1775 – Second Continental Congress; Allen and Armold capture Fort Ticonderoga

18 May 1775 – Abercrombie's reconnaissance up the Charles River

25 May 1775 – Arrival of Howe, Clinton and Burgoyne aboard the *Cerberus*

28 May 1775 – Battle on Noddle's Island

12 June 1775 – Gage declares martial law and offers a pardon to all rebels except Adams and Hancock

15 June 1775 – Washington made commander-in-chief; British plan of attack discovered

16-17 JUNE BATTLE OF BREED'S (BUNKER'S) HILL

0900 – Council of War meets to discuss reply to British plan of attack; matter passed to Ward

2100 – Prescott's Massachusetts contingent leave Cambridge Common, gathering Putnam, Knowlton's contingent and entrenching tools on the way

2400 – Prescott arrives on Bunker's Hill; argument over which hill to defend

0400 – Lookouts aboard the *Lively* spot the American works on Breed's Hill and she opens fire

0700 – British council of war ends having decided on an amphibious assault on Charlestown peninsula

1200 – American detachments occupy abandoned buildings in Charlestown

1300 – British first wave leaves Boston wharves; Ward sends nine Massachusetts and two New Hampshire regiments to support Prescott

1400 – British first wave lands; Prescott sends Knowlton to delay them

1500 – Howe lands with second British wave; Stark arrives at rail fence to reinforce Knowlton

1530 – Light infantry repulsed by Stark; Howe's first attack fails against the rail fence and falls back

1600 – Howe's second attack against the rail fence; Pigott's feint against the redoubt

1630 – Clinton sends reinforcements; Howe's final attack all along the American line is launched

1700 – Pigott's troops capture the redoubt; Clinton arrives and takes over the pursuit of the fleeing enemy

1730 – Pigott's light companies encounter the American rearguard

1800 – Clinton reaches Charlestown Neck and orders his men to halt; Americans keep British under desultory fire

2300 – The *Lively* quickly disperses American forces forming up to attack Charlestown Neck

EVENTS LEADING UP TO THE BRITISH EVACUATION OF BOSTON

18 June 1775 – British fortify Charlestown peninsula

31 July 1775 – Americans destroy lighthouse on Great Brewster Island

26 August 1775 – Americans fortify Ploughed Hill during the night

28 August 1775 – Expedition against Canada begins

9 November 1775 – British raid on Lechmere Point

23 November 1775 – Americans fortify Cobble Hill during the night

9 December 1775 – Skirmish at Great Bridge, Virginia

31 December 1775 – Two-day assault on Quebec begins

8 January 1776 – Americans attack Charlestown during performance of Burgoyne's play 'The Blockade of Boston'

25 January 1776 – Knox and his artillery arrive in Cambridge

27 February 1776 – Battle at Moore's Creek Bridge, North Carolina

4 March 1776 – Americans fortify Dorchester Heights during the night

17 March 1776 – Evacuation of Boston garrison to Halifax

A GUIDE TO FURTHER READING

History is invariably written by the winners and rarely more obviously so than in this conflict. While the 1975 bicentennial was a watershed for revisionist American historians, in Great Britain the legends still endure (much as with the First World War), and not surprisingly the most sympathetic views of British policy and strategy are mostly found in American works.

The books listed below are specific to this campaign and their bibliographies include the better-known general texts also consulted. Publication dates are of those editions used by the author.

On the background and causes of the war: *Miller, J. -Origins of the American Revolution, London, 1945;* and *Hibbert, C. – Redcoats and Rebels, London, 1990.* For a (pro-American) general military history of the conflict: *Ward, C. – The War of the Revolution, New York, 1952.*

On garrison life in colonial Boston: *Barker, J. – The British in Boston, New York, 1969;* and *MacKenzie, F. – The Diary of Frederick MacKenzie, Cambridge, 1930.*

On the opposing commanders: *Boatner, M. – Cassell's Biographical Dictionary of the American War of Independence, London, 1974;* and the *Dictionary of National Biography, London 1960;* both provide good detail, especially on the important, but less well known characters.

On the opposing forces, the following cover the Army in colonial North America, and its organisation and command structure: *Shy, J. – Toward Lexington: The role of the British Army in the Coming of the American Revolution, Princeton University, 1965;* and *Curtis, E. – The Organisation of the British Army in the Revolution, Wakefield, 1972.* For the American forces: *Galvin, Major General J. – The Minute Men, New York, 1989;* gives an excellent analysis of the Massachusetts militia and its actual – as opposed to mythical – capabilities. *Wright, R. – The Continental Army, Washington, 1989;* charts the evolution of the first national army. *Higginbotham, D. – The War of American Independence, New York, 1971;* considers American military policy and social attitudes towards military service, prior to the outbreak of war.

On the events of 19 April: *Tourtellot, A. – William Diamond's Drum,*

New York, 1960; is the latest – and probably most accurate – account, and also provides fascinating social background. *French, A. – Day of Lexington and Concord, Boston, 1925;* has been superceded by subsequent research, but manages to be objective and realistic.

For the events of 17 June (and before): *Elting, Colonel J. – The Battle of Bunker's Hill, Monmouth Beach, 1975;* shows a professional soldier's understanding of military problems often overlooked by 'armchair' tacticians. Also: *Fleming, T. – Now We Are Enemies, New York, 1960; and Ketchum, R. – The Battle for Bunker Hill, London, 1962;* both dramatised accounts.

On the siege of Boston: *Frothingham, R. – History of The Siege of Boston, Boston, 1851;* good, but somewhat dated. Also: *Russell, F. – Lexington, Concord and Bunker Hill, Mahwah (NJ), 1963;* a modern view and an excellent basic 'primer', despite being aimed at younger readers.

For maps and charts: *Marshall, W. and Peckham, H. -Campaigns of the American Revolution, New Jersey, 1976.* Also: *Symonds, C. and Clipson, W. – A Battlefield Atlas of the American Revolution, Anapolis, 1986.*

WARGAMING THE BOSTON CAMPAIGN

Wargaming (or historical simulation) is the hobby of refighting the campaigns of history, or fighting fictitious battles in an historical context, using model soldiers and terrain, counters on maps, or 'role-play'. This is not the place to discuss the mechanics of the hobby in any detail (numerous introductory books are available for those new to the hobby), but as this is the first *Campaign* book on a Revolutionary battle, some general comments about the conflict may be useful.

The Revolution does not enjoy the widespread popularity of other 'horse-and-musket' periods, such as the Napoleonic Wars, despite a potential appeal to British and American audiences (who comprise about 90 per cent of the world's wargamers), and the availability of information on both sides in English. Enduring mythology concerning British inflexibility and poor generalship, suggest that a truly authentic set of rules leave them no chance of winning; equally, a more liberal set – and the benefit of hindsight – make them unbeatable. The resulting lack of interest makes the period uneconomical for rule-writers and figure makers, who generally ignore it (unless they have a personal interest). This is a shame, as even a superficial glance discloses many engagements much better suited to the average wargamer's limited resources than Napoleonic 'classics', and can be replayed in different formats – solo, 'free kriegsspiel', committee games, role-play, or straight figure games – according to taste.

The mention of figures leads to another general comment. Napleon said, 'a battalion often decides the day', but in the American Revolution, it was usually a company, or troop. The war offers a rare middle-ground between the major set-piece battle and the small skirmish, with few engagements having more than 5000 men per side. This allows wargamers the opportunity of a 'horse-and-musket' army with large units (using figure:man ratios as low as 1:10, 1:5, or even 1:1) and deploying substantial numbers of 25mm figures, with their extra detail and 'character', without breaking the bank – or the table!

With the right rules, wargamers can acquire the working knowledge of small unit tactics and manoeuvres that was essential to officers on both sides, and which make hitherto obscure (or even absurd) decisions easier to understand. The Concord raid, for example, would require only 400 figures to represent both sides at a ratio of 1:10 – far lower than is feasible for most Napoleonic battles. Obviously, the time and money needed to build this miniature force must be considered, but since virtually every unit can be re-used in later campaigns, it will almost certainly prove to be an excellent investment.

COMMITTEE OF SAFETY

For those interested in administration and logistics, the operations of the Committees of Safety and Supplies offer an opportunity for a committee game. Player briefings should be loosely based on historical characters, but with fictitious names and certain obvious traits altered to avoid identification (as one of the committee must be a spy). The Committee is given a map of Massachusetts and decides where to hide stores and weapons; how and when to issue them; and creates an 'early warning' system to prevent Gage from seizing them – each town should also have a 'Tory factor', to determine how secure it is.

Obviously, the further stores are from Boston, the longer they take to arrive if needed, but the safer they are from Gage; the umpire can prevent the players from overloading remote towns by 'stacking' or points limits, or introducing sudden 'emergencies'. Players should have individual responsibilities, and how much of these they reveal to other players will determine how much of the overall picture Gage receives from his spy. The spy is naturally playing a different game, and must try to send Gage as much information as possible (through the umpire in writing) without being caught.

BOSTON GARRISON

This is a multi-player role-playing game (an umpire – well-read in the period – is also essential) with one player as Gage, and the others representing Bostonians and British officers. The game depicts Gage's struggle to keep order in Boston, while retaining the respect of his troops. Using a calendar and historical events selected from various diaries and memoirs, the umpire traces the period from Gage's arrival in Boston as Governor of Massachusetts, to the outbreak of war (which may come sooner, or later, than in reality). Mob violence, letters home from officers with political connections, street-fights, spies, thefts of military stores and arguments with Graves, should all be sent to try the 'Gage' player, whose responses (from a 'menu' of likely options) are put to the others who can plead, threaten or cajol, as the fancy takes them.

The umpire, using 'free kriegsspiel', decides the likely consequences of Gage's decisions and, taking account of the other players' reactions, plots the results on two charts – one marked 'public order', the other 'garrison morale'. A positive decision on one chart will usually, but not always, produce a negative reaction on the other. Gage must try to keep both sides happy for as long as possible; failure to do so means either war or mutiny,

The view across Lexington Green today, with the road off to Concord at the left. The statue commemorates Captain Parker, and the stone behind the statue, and in front of the flagpole marks the site of the three-storey meeting house shown in all contemporary views of the common. (Author's photograph)

and his recall to England – lasting beyond 19 April can be considered a victory.

As an addendum to this game, a quick one-player game could have a British colonel marching his regiment into the countryside (either on a specific mission, for example to seize stores, or just to train) and being shadowed by umpire-generated groups of militia. The player must follow orders as closely as possible, keep his men under control (and retain their respect), but must also avoid bloodshed and, above all else, must not fire the first shots. Every successful march earns points, but the more marches attempted, the more hostile the response and the more likely a 'mission' will be requested by Gage. The marches become increasingly difficult, in terms of militia hostility – militia units are chosen by the umpire from a roster, with randomly-generated morale, discipline and leaders (either 'doves' or anti-British 'hawks'). The militia will also become bolder and more confident each time the regulars back down from a confrontation, making each successive march more difficult.

The regiment must march regularly, or it becomes unfit for active service and causes trouble in Boston (which affects morale and earns the player damaging 'mentions' in Whig newspapers in Boston and London). The objective is to keep the regiment in good order, well-trained and disciplined and the player is responsible for day-to-day administration. The umpire will give frequent situation reports, to which the player must respond by choosing from a given menu of orders and the game runs from 1 January 1775 until blood is shed, or until 19 April, when war is deemed to break out.

ALARM RIDERS

Another role-play game involves the activities of the 'alarm riders'. The date is 18 April, 1775, and the players are either the riders — with an option to play historical characters, such as Revere — or the British patrols sent out to intercept them (in either case, the umpire controls the other side).

Each rider chooses a pre-selected route and wins points for avoiding — or escaping — patrols, and the number and military importance of any inhabitants 'roused' (whose homes are plotted on the umpire's master map, but not divulged to the players). Delays and confusion can be generated by 'sightings' of anonymous riders under trees or in fields; equally, a patrol may (on the umpire's say so) allow a captured rider to go after a number of moves have elapsed.

Alternatively, the players may take the role of British officers — either as individual patrol leaders, such as Major Mitchell, or as members of the same group (giving a committee game). It must be emphasised that the object is merely to prevent the riders warning the countryside ahead of Smith's column, not to kill them (though one or more players may be encouraged to take a dim view of the 'damned rebels' and Gage's concern for their liberties). Points are awarded for any riders captured (or forced to deviate from their routes); they can be interrogated, but the umpire must ensure that contemporary attitudes and standards of behaviour are observed. The umpire may even introduce completely innocent civilians to add further confusion. The patrols must try to rendezvous with Smith's column, at which point the game ends.

Special rules should allow for the riders' superior knowledge of the roads (though not necessarily the area as a whole), while the British should be handicapped by uncertainty over how aggressive they can be — when can they use their weapons? Is it better to allow a rider to escape, or risk shooting an innocent man?

LEXINGTON AND CONCORD

The events of 19 April are not conducive to 'decision-making' games, as few 'decisions' were made that day, except to retreat (British) and harass (American), though the confusion among the British company commanders at North Bridge might make an interesting committee or role-play 'opener' to a figure game.

It is debatable whether the incident at Lexington is worth recreating, as it was a small and inevitably one-sided affair, whose only variable would be the casualties on each side. However, the incidents at Concord and the return to Boston can be reconstructed using a team to play the various British commanders: Smith, Pitcairn, Pole, Parsons, Laurie and Percy (who should make his preparations 'off-table' — ie, in another room).

The militia can be umpire-generated (using historical data, varied slightly to avoid British hindsight). If no umpire is available, use a suitably modified version of the system of generating the Indians in Ian Beck's excellent *Pony Wars* rules by Tabletop Games; it is important to keep a tally of how many men are engaged (no more than 2000 militia were attacking at any one time) and ammunition expenditure, which forced several companies out of the fighting later on.

If a lot of players are available, it would be possible to have the umpire control the British (sending out flankers when appropriate, but generally marching along the table), while the players command individual militia companies, choosing tactics and ambush positions. The column should 'shed' casualties along the road, with each player scoring points for how many regulars his company hits, less his own losses. The effect of their firing should be hidden behind cotton wool 'smoke' and 'dust' and the umpire should keep losses realistically low, while giving encouraging reports to the players (who will learn at the end that, as in reality, they did not hit as many regulars as they thought).

The table-top terrain, should consist of a long narrow table (or set of tables), with the game played along its length. As the battlefield was 20 miles long and rarely more than 200 yards wide, the British column should 'move' by 'rolling' the terrain beneath it, from front to rear. Both games can benefit from seating the players so as to have the table at eye level (thereby denying a 'God-like' view of the battlefield) and when the British are played, the table could be split in half, lengthwise, so that the players effectively sit in the middle of the road, with views to either side.

An alternative game for the Americans would be to have the players represent a group of 'minute men'; each player would have a points quota to spend on weapons and personal abilities, and would have to act as part of a team (the other players are his friends and neighbours – possibly even his family – as well as comrades in arms, after all). The umpire should keep a close watch on ammunition expenditure and on British flanking parties creeping up behind them.

BREED'S HILL

Moving to the events of 17 June, an intriguing 'committee game' could be devised around Ward's council of war of 16 June, and the ensuing confusion over whether Bunker's or Breed's Hills should be fortified. Players could be specially chosen to match their personal characteristics with those of Ward, Prescott, Putnam, et al, with points being awarded for making events follow their character's intentions. The umpire could also throw in some 'what if' scenarios – for example, British sentries hearing them digging – requiring instant decision-taking.

Gage's council of war later that morning offers similar possibilities for a committee game. Players represent the British Army and Royal Navy officers, and their staffs, again trying to match the traits of players and historical characters. A strict time limit should be observed for this game and the winner is the player whose plan to dislodge the Americans is finally adopted – it could even be played out on the table-top, as a 'what if' scenario.

The most obvious format for recreating the fighting on Charlestown peninsula is a figure game, but with several important factors to be taken into account. First, the British player must not know the terrain in front of him – if an umpire is available, that part of the table can be left bare, or covered with false terrain, allowing the player to find the obstacles the hard way; if not, the player generates the obstacles by a die-roll each time a unit moves forward. Second, the light infantry must be forced to advance along the beach as if they are unaware of Stark, behind the wall; to add interest to this, variables can be introduced to the fire and morale of Stark's men, giving a determined British attack some chance of success. Care is also needed over the morale of the Massachusetts units; some did nothing, but others did well and should be allowed to stand and fight. The British displayed extraordinarily high morale throughout, but unusually poor musketry and fire-discipline – no 'plus one for British infantry firing' here!

If the umpire/organiser feels that such a game is too predictable, why not create a 'disguised scenario', by transferring the battle to another place and time? Boston 1775 could become Bengal 1795, with a smaller British force against the semi-trained masses of a Nabob, holding incomplete defences and with a massive, but unreliable, reserve. Such a scenario would allow similar sets of rules and orders-of-battle to be used, and should fool all but the most knowledgeable player.

THE SIEGE

Another use for 'disguised scenarios' in figure wargames would be the fighting on the islands around the harbour, such as the raid on Noddle's Island on 28 May, with troops fighting waist-deep in water and the intervention – and possible capture – of a small warship; the destruction of the lighthouse and the working party sent to repair it; British foraging raids in the winter; or the night-time occupation of Dorchester Heights and other hills around Boston (including 'what if' British counter attacks).

The siege itself can be recreated as a simple 'map', or 'table', campaign game between two armies, but this could easily acquire an unrealistic level of co-ordination (especially with only one or two players per side). Alternatively, an individual, or team, controls one army (and the umpire the other) and 'role-plays' the leaders – fighting each other as often as the enemy. Each player would be briefed on his historical character, and has to undertake administrative, as well as military, functions. Victory conditions could reflect personal achievements, as well as (in some cases instead of) collective ones.

The umpire may introduce logistical and political problems – for example, inter-colonial rivalry; disease and desertion; expiry of enlistment terms; and the arrival of British reinforcements. Given the possibility of random (or umpire-generated) deviation, the real timetable of events could control the game, with unexpected delays preventing total predictability. Weather was also important, on land and at sea (a splendid 'what if' battle would result from an American attack over the ice). Weather generation can either use historical data (such as Nathaniel Ames', *An Astronomical Diary*), dice, or modern records – last year's forecasts for the Boston area, for example.